Homepage and Splashpage

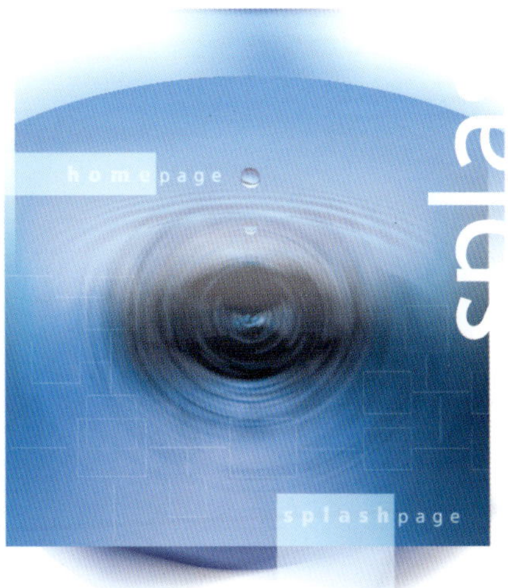

WEB SITE GRAPHICS

The Best Work from the Web

by RICHARD KARL DANIELSON

GLOUCESTER MASSACHUSETTS

ROCKPORT PUBLISHERS

First published in the United States of America by:
Rockport Publishers, Inc.
33 Commercial Street
Gloucester, Massachusetts 01930-5089
Telephone
(978) 282-9590
Facsimile
(978) 283-2742
www.rockpub.com

ISBN 1-56496-723-9

10 9 8 7 6 5 4 3 2 1

Designer: Daniel Donnelly
Layout: Cathy Kelley Graphic Design
Cover Image: Madison Design and Advertising

Printed in China.

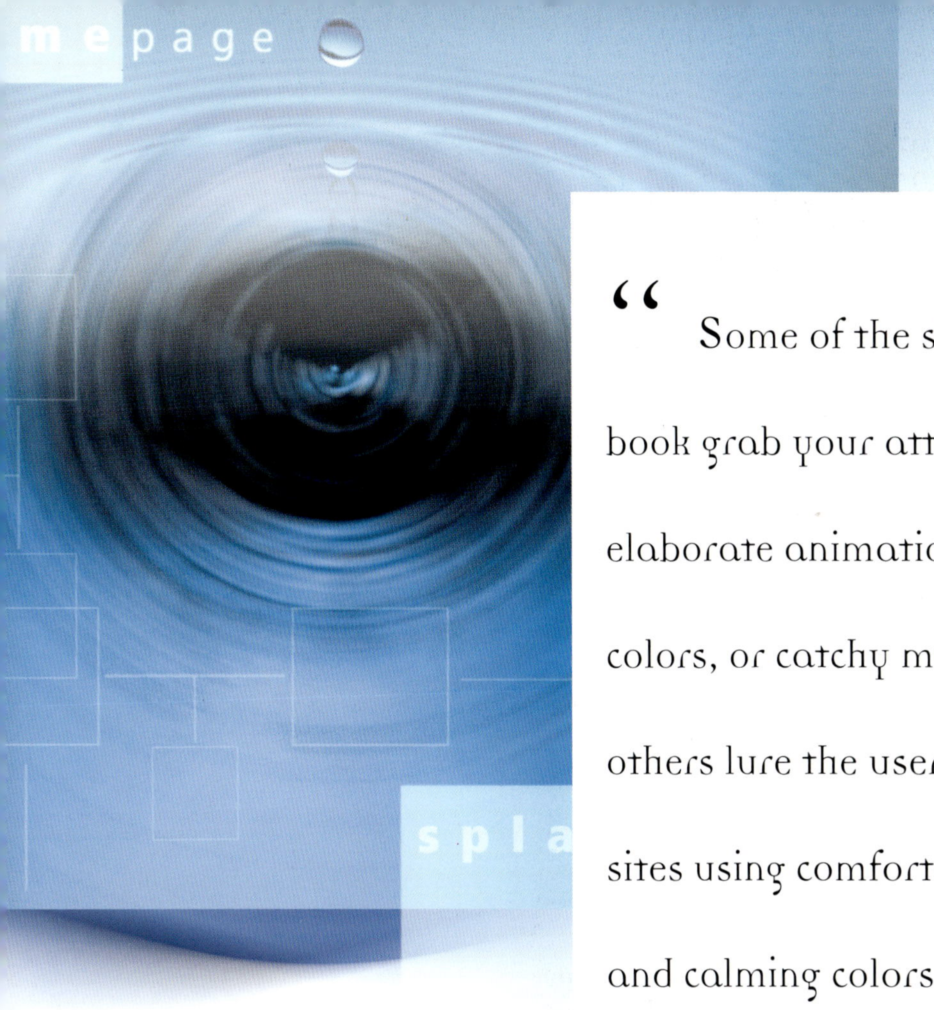

"Some of the sites in this book grab your attention with elaborate animations, bright colors, or catchy music, while others lure the user into their sites using comfortable design and calming colors. It doesn't matter how you do it; the point is to keep the user at your site."

introduction

The cliché goes: You only get one chance to make a first impression.

That is true of the Internet even more than in most of life. It only takes a few seconds for a viewer to click away from your site. How does a designer keep users from moving on?

Some of the sites in this book grab your attention with elaborate animations, bright colors, or catchy music, while others lure the user into their sites using comfortable design and calming colors. It doesn't matter how you do it; the point is to keep the user at your site.

Recent innovations in Internet technology have opened up new options to designers everywhere. Chief among these is Macromedia's Flash, which has allowed a whole new age of moving pictures, but none of this would be possible without the continuing strides in bandwidth. Just a few years ago, most home users used 11K modems; now, just about everyone is up to 56K, with millions of people already connected via DSL and cable modems. The growth of high-speed Internet connections will break down the remaining barriers in Web design. The Internet color palette will continue to expand. Web sites will feature true soundtracks and songs. Animation and even streaming movies will be possible and all of this will download in seconds.

The common denominator among the sites featured in this book is the excellence of design. Design is all around us. We can either take notice or allow it to wash over us. I would argue that an unexamined design life is a life strongly diminished.

The world is in the midst of what I would call a design renaissance. The iMac and the new Volkswagen Beetle, along with the types of Web sites featured in this book, are defining a modern design sensibility the likes of which we haven't seen in this country since the Art Deco period.

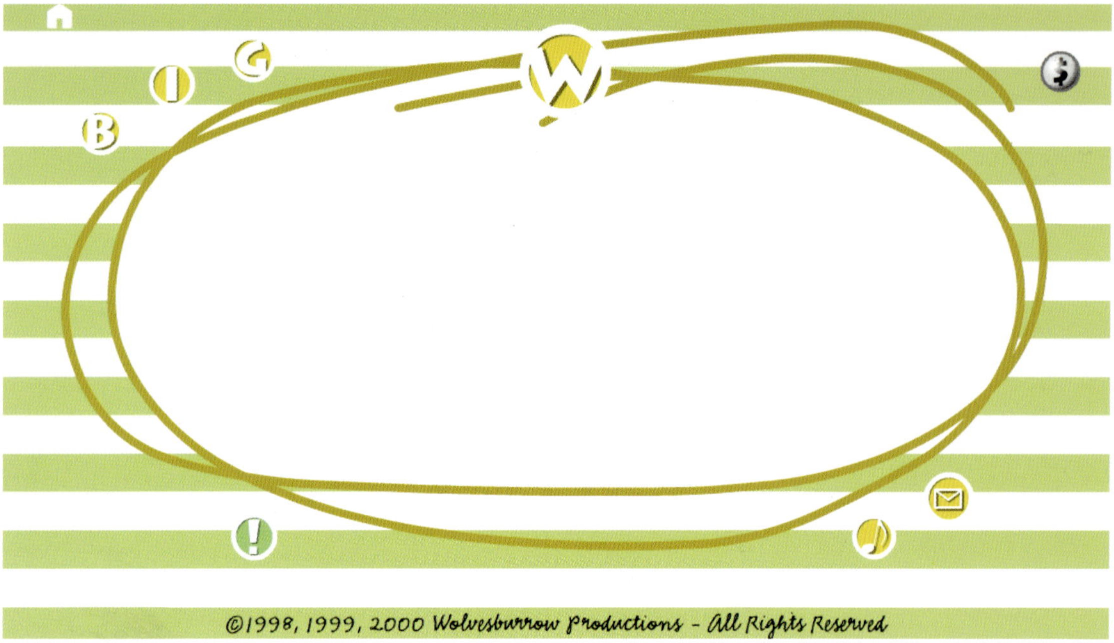

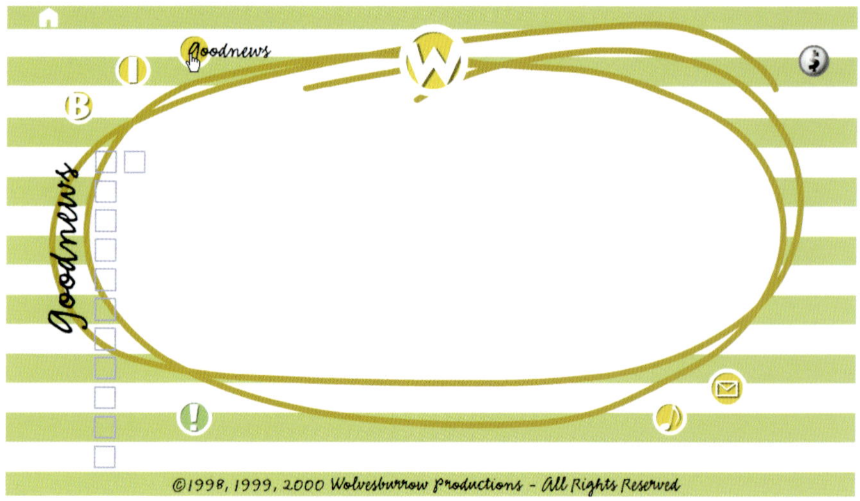

Title
wolvesburrow
URL
www.wolvesburrow.com/
Design firm
wolvesburrow productions

The Wolvesburrow site has a look you don't see very often on the Internet. The horizontal stripes and the pale yellow color create a look more often seen in print media. "What matters most is that we won't crash you," is what they say at Wolvesburrow.

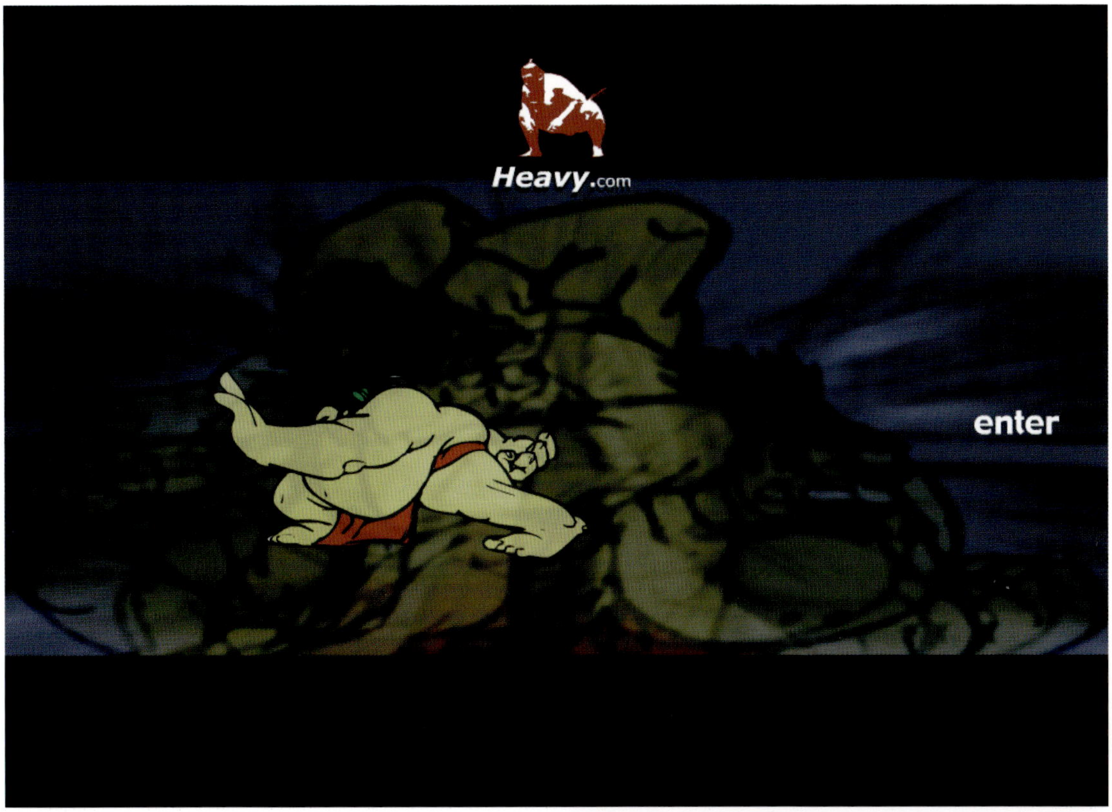

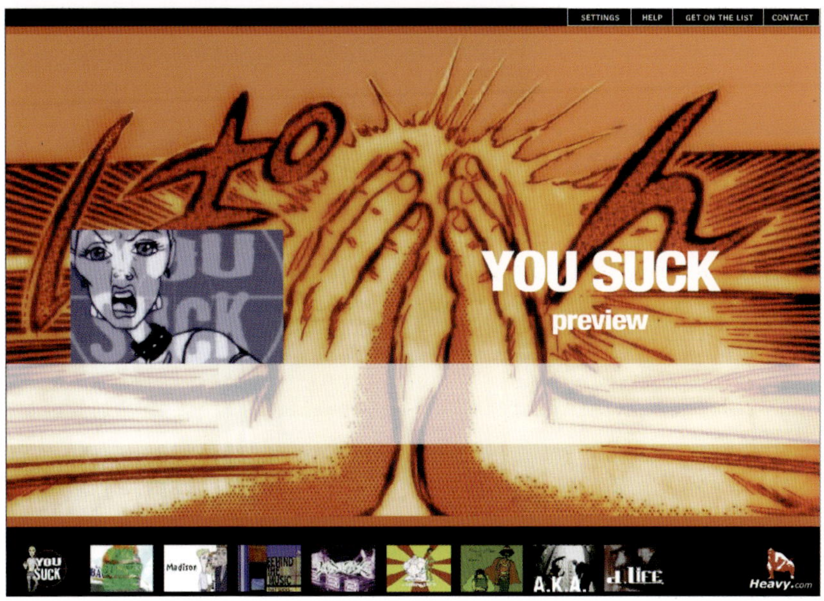

Title
Heavy.com
URL
www.heavy.com/
Design firm
Heavy.com

The centerpiece of this splashpage is the excellent illustration. The navigation bar is Flash-animated, giving their splashpage a cool, cutting-edge look.

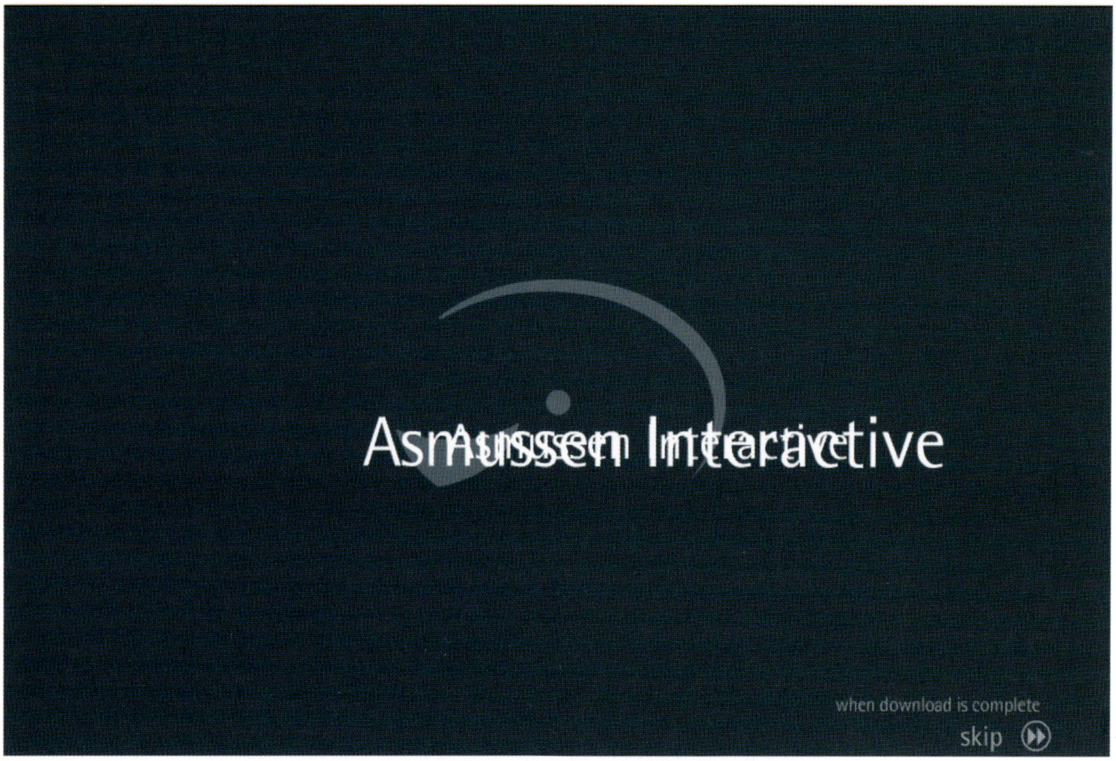

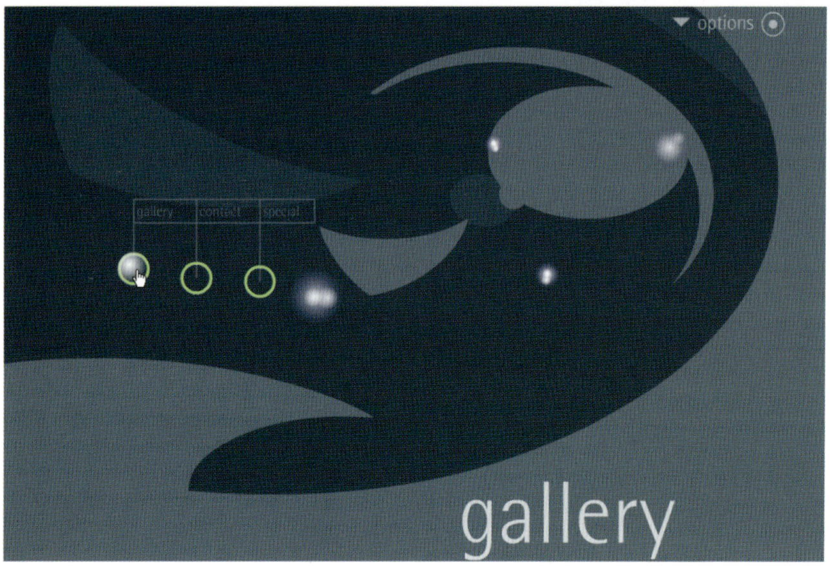

Title
Asmussen Interactive
URL
www.turtleshell.com/asm
Design Firm
Asmussen Interactive

The painter's hand logo in the corner of this page is the first thing that draws your attention. Stars float across the screen, creating a serene effect to match the cool blue color scheme.

Title

gary venter

URL

www.gva.net.au/

Design firm

gary venter Architect

One simple image is repeated—the designer's face. The eyes move around, looking up, down, and right at you. This is a cool, and somewhat creepy, homepage.

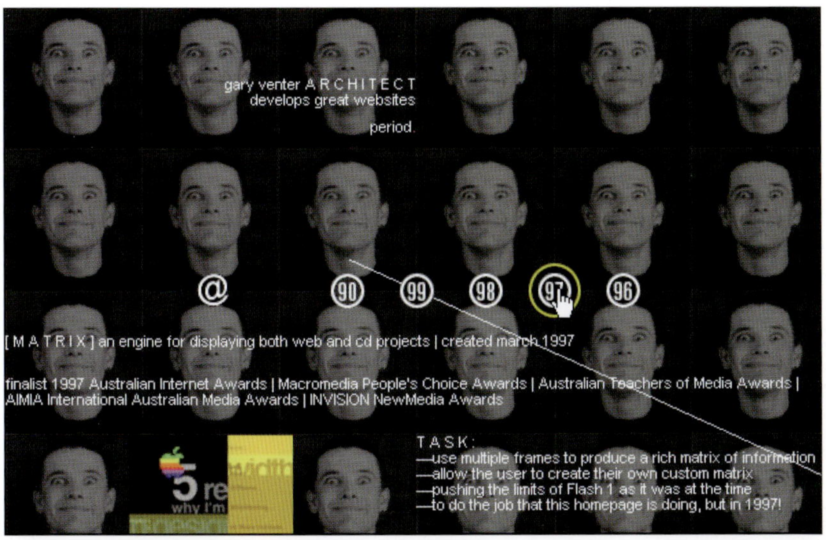

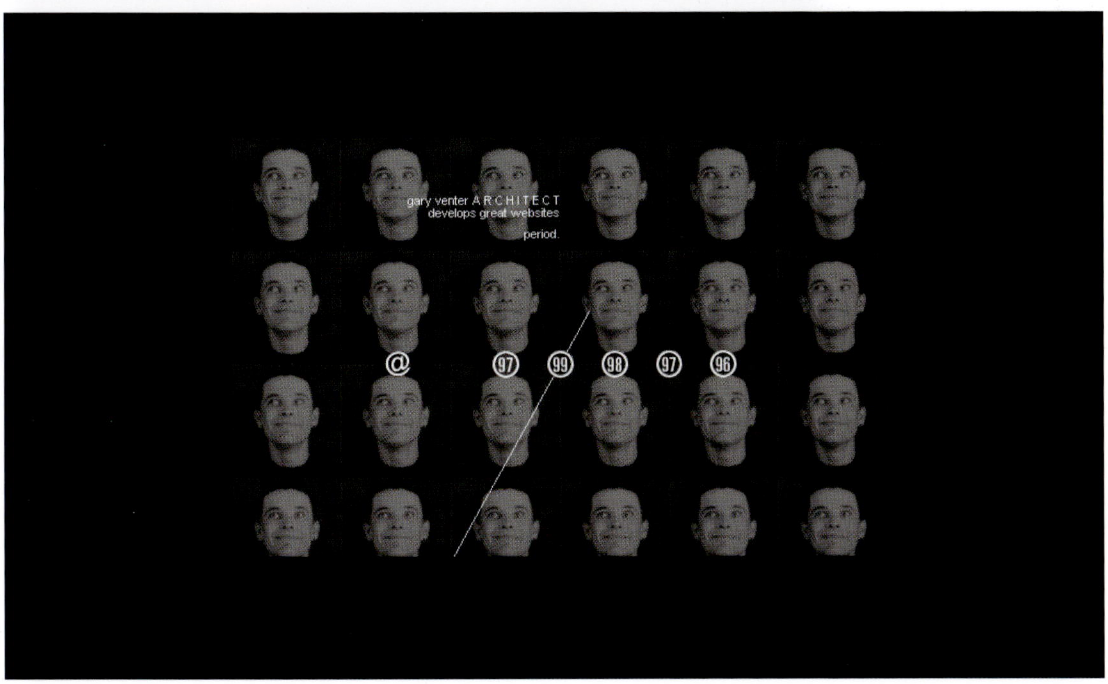

Title
Lambie-Nairn
URL
www.lambie-nairn.com/flash_go.html
Design Firm
Lambie-Nairn

The Lambie-Nairn homepage makes excellent use of negative space. This sparsely decorated site gives you just the information you want in a creative way. Click on one of the buttons along the right side; the box slides open over the button to reveal the information you requested. Click on the slide bar below the box to view the images of Lambie-Nairn's work.

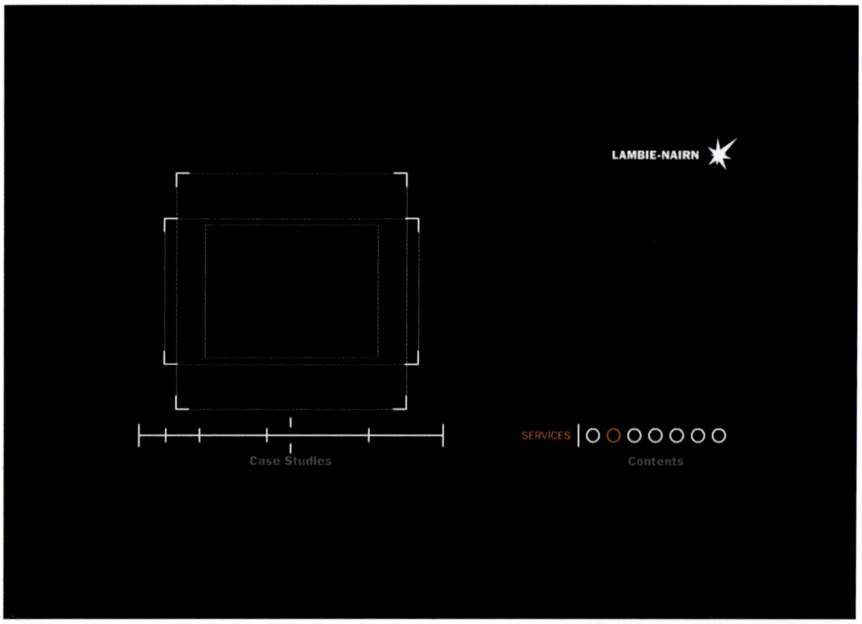

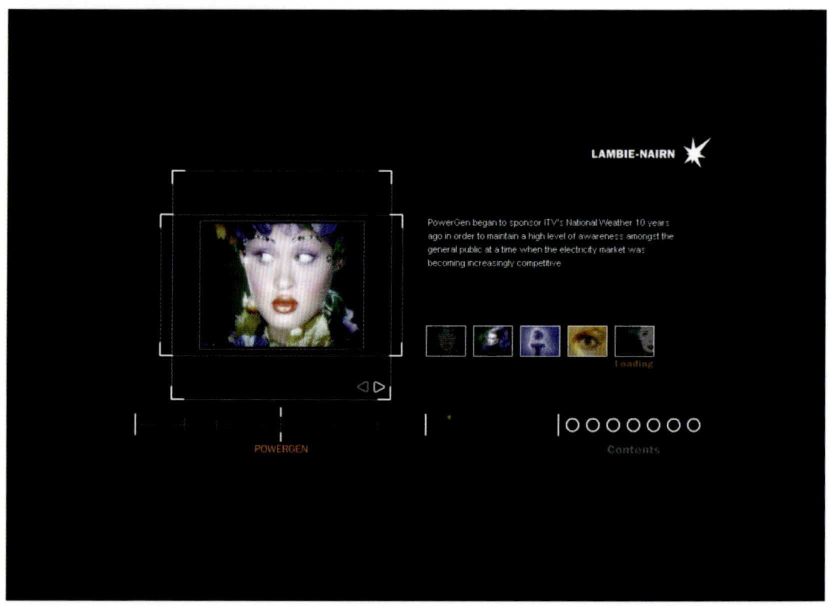

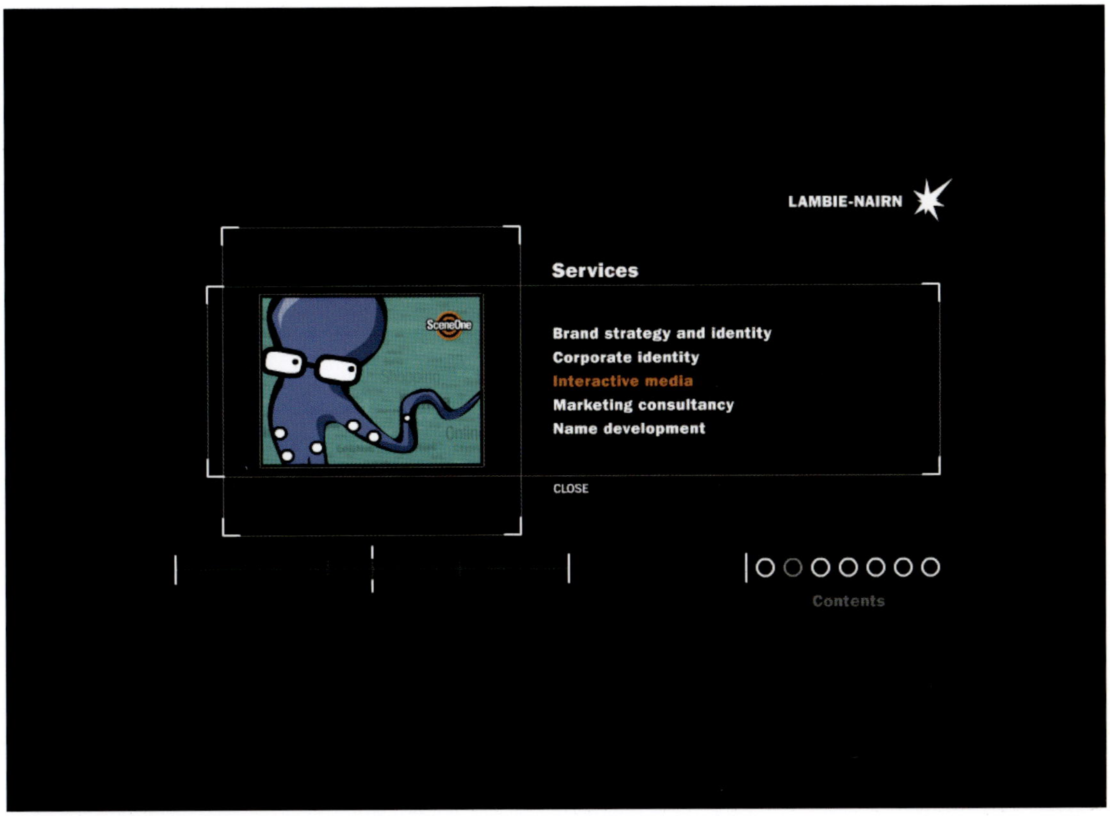
LAMBIE-NAIRN
Services
SceneOne
Brand strategy and identity
Corporate identity
Interactive media
Marketing consultancy
Name development
CLOSE
Contents

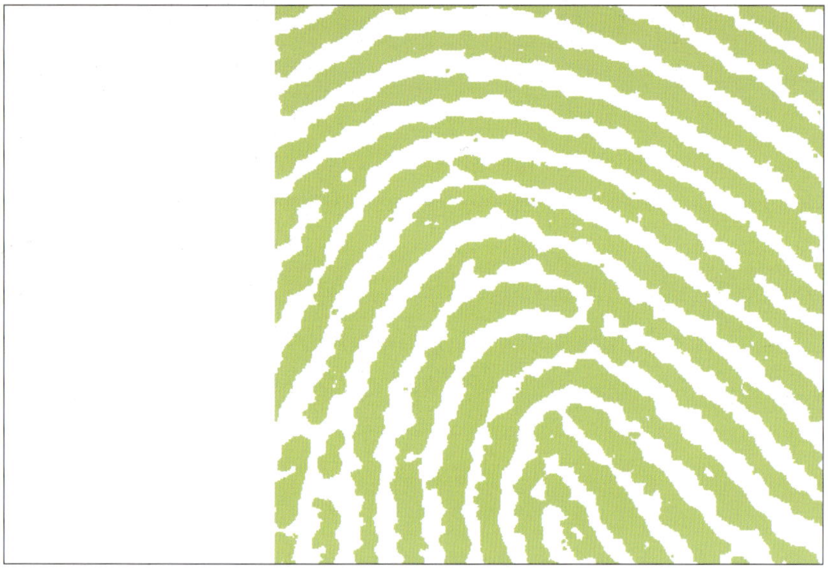

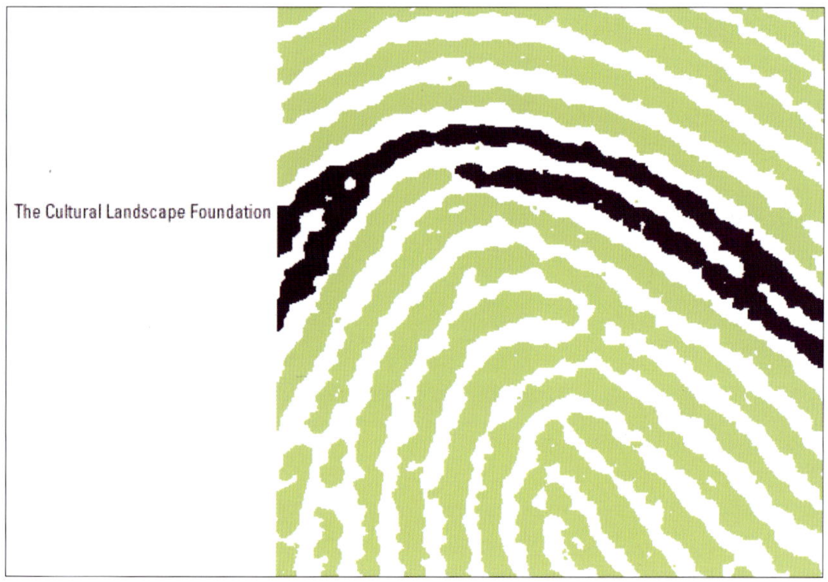

Title
Cultural Landscape Foundation
URL
www.tclf.org/
Design Firm
Coleman Design Group
Designer
Richard Benson

The Cultural Landscape Foundation homepage features colors not generally seen on the Internet. The compelling images and unobtrusive buttons combine to make a lovely homepage.

The Cultural Landscape Foundation

Cultural landscapes give us a sense of place. They are part of our national heritage, and part of each of our lives. They reveal our relationship with the land over time. As with historic buildings, cultural landscapes are special places that reveal aspects of our country's origin and development through their forms, features, and history of use.

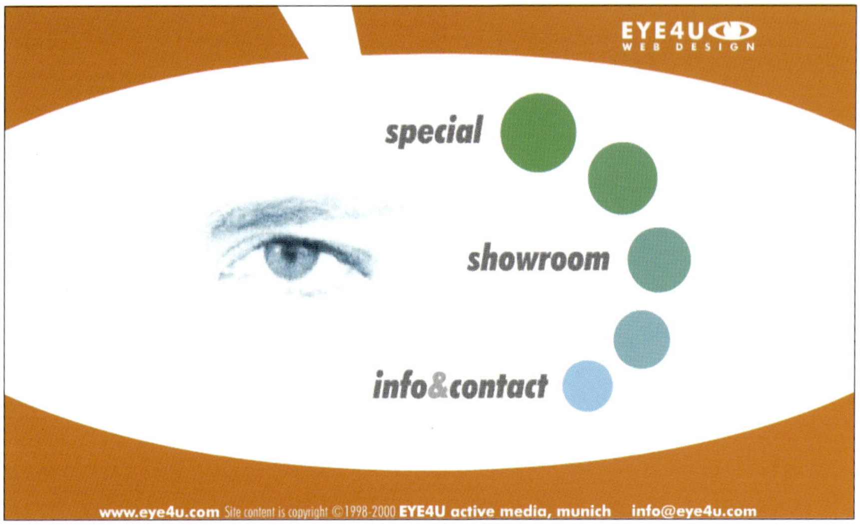

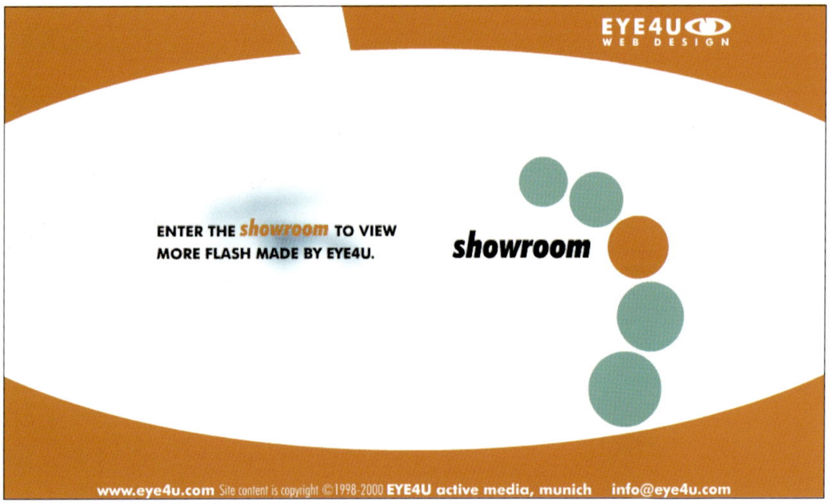

Title
Eye4U
URL
eye4u.com/home/index.htm
Design Firm
Eye 4 U Active Media

The Eye4U site uses Flash extensively to create a splashpage with animation. The extensive movement and sound take a few seconds to load, but are well worth it. Eye4U credits their background in television production for creating an almost movielike experience.

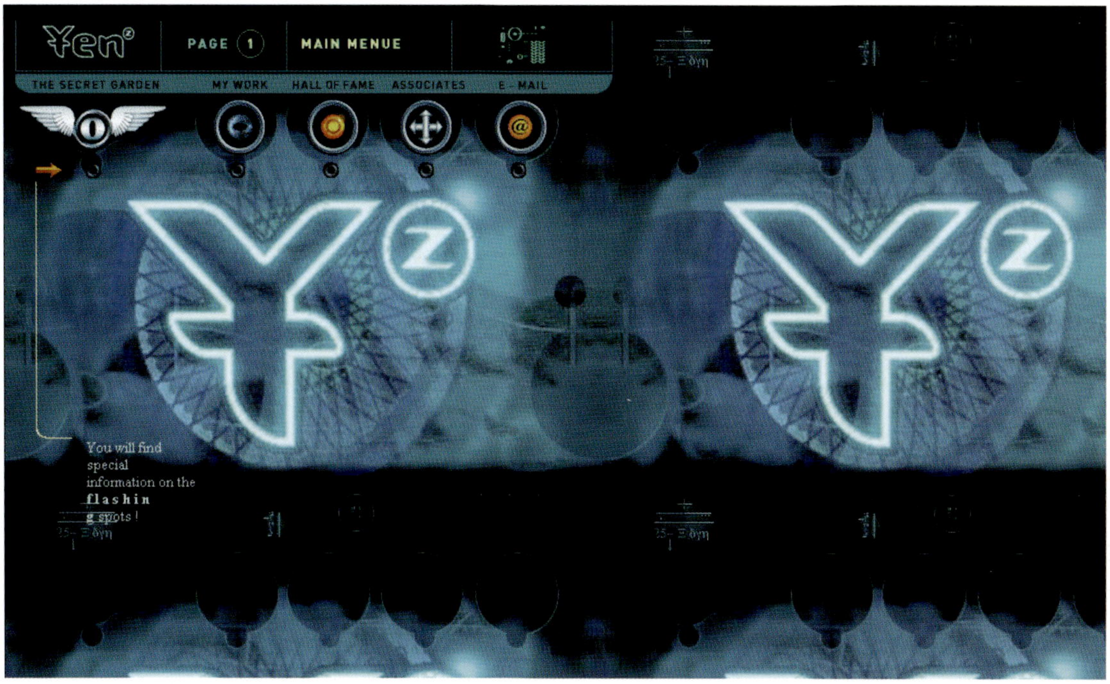

Title
Yenz/The Secret Garden
URL
www.yenz.com/
Design Firm
Yenz
Programmer
kosmokrator.com

Yenz is one of the most stunning sites on the Internet. Lush illustrations and a modern look combine to draw you into the site immediately.

Title
staticlife

URL
www.staticlife.com/box/1998/html

Design firm
Todaiflunk No-Media Network

This homepage does a great job of introducing you to this art-for-art's-sake site. The multimedia design has a modern feel with ambiguous buttons and jarringly juxtaposed images.

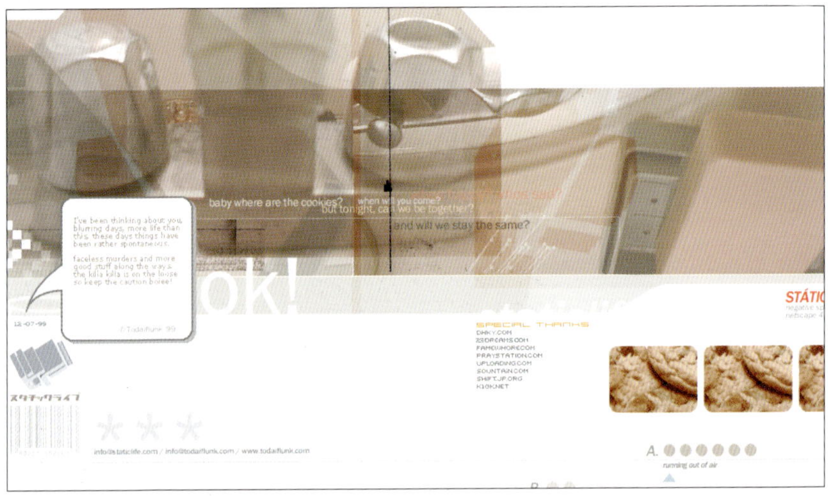

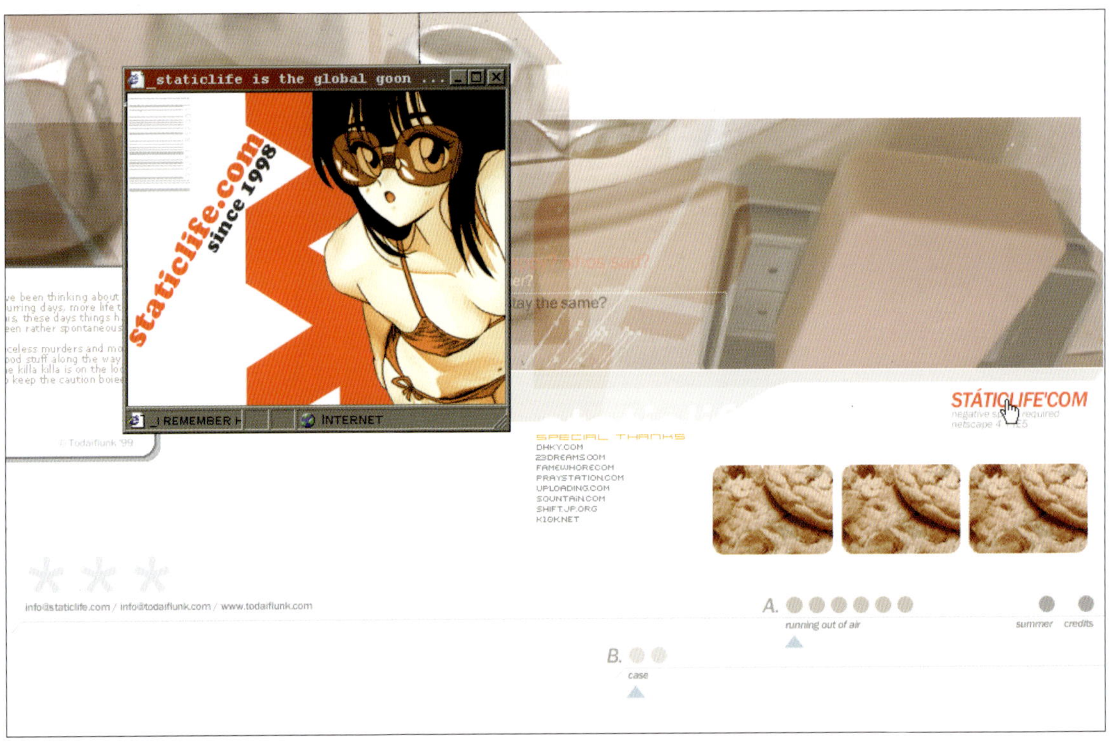

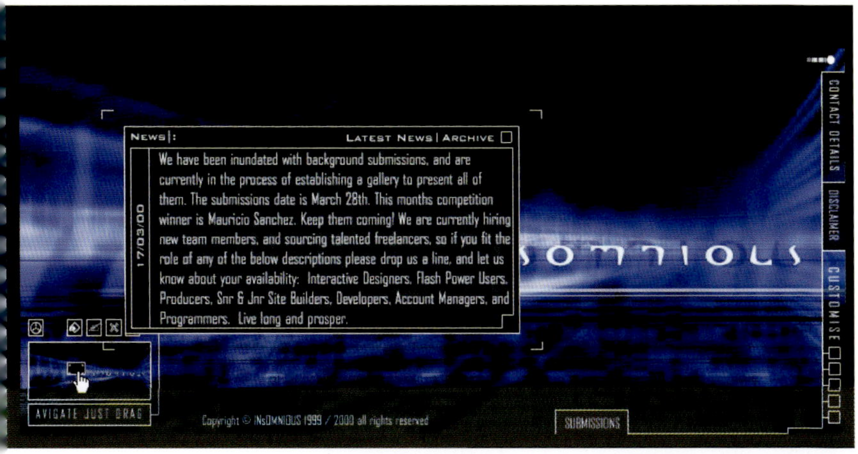

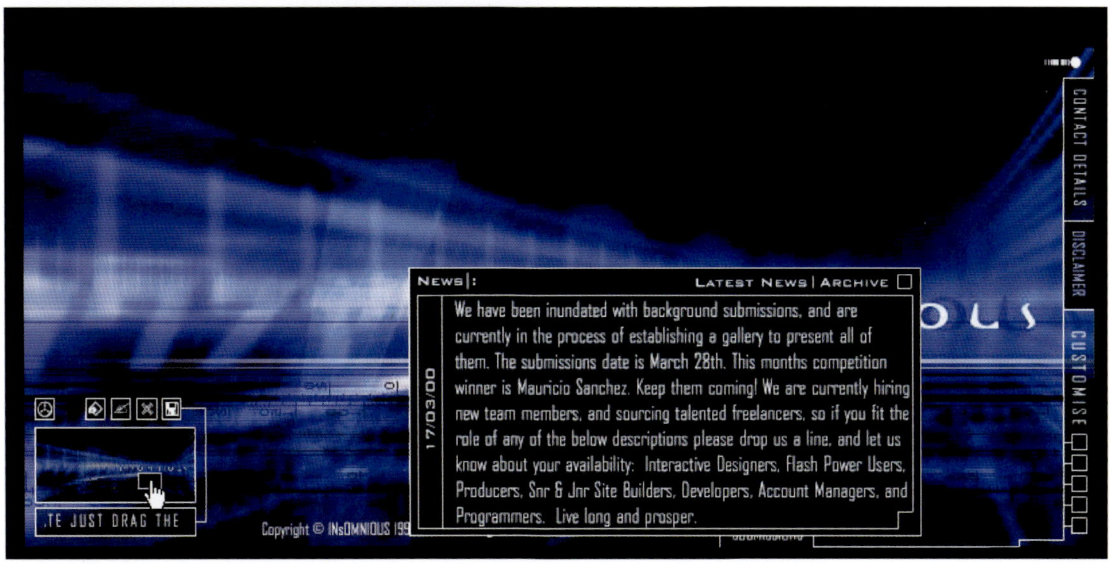

Title
Insomnious
URL
www.insomnious.com/
Design firm
Insomnious, Ltd.

The Insomnious homepage pushes the limits of Web design. Using Flash, Insomnious created an original interface with four buttons that you pull down into a small box that is mimicked by the information. You can also change the background images.

Title
Ntouch
URL
ntouch.linst.ac.uk/
Design firm
Random Media

The Ntouch homepage features a blue and orange color scheme not often seen on the Web. The eight buttons that reveal their function on mouse-over are cleverly constructed to look like Chinese characters.

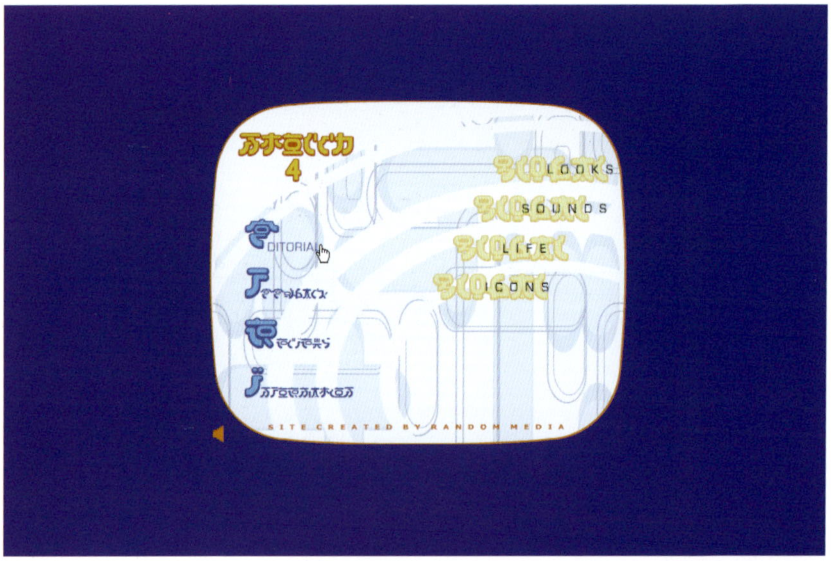

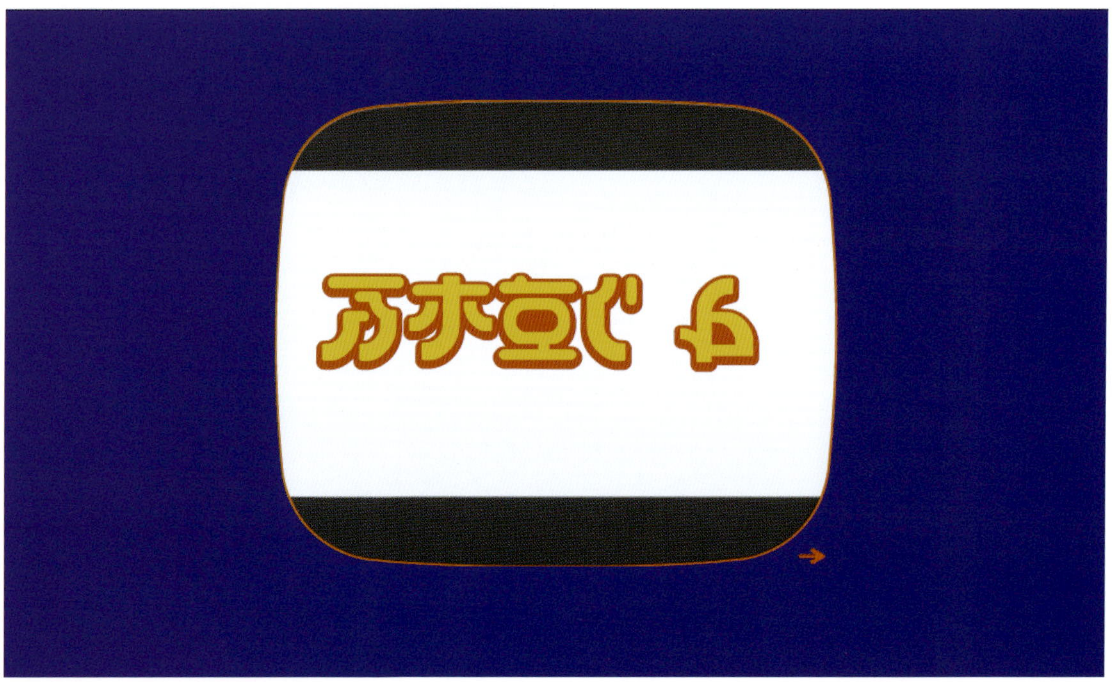

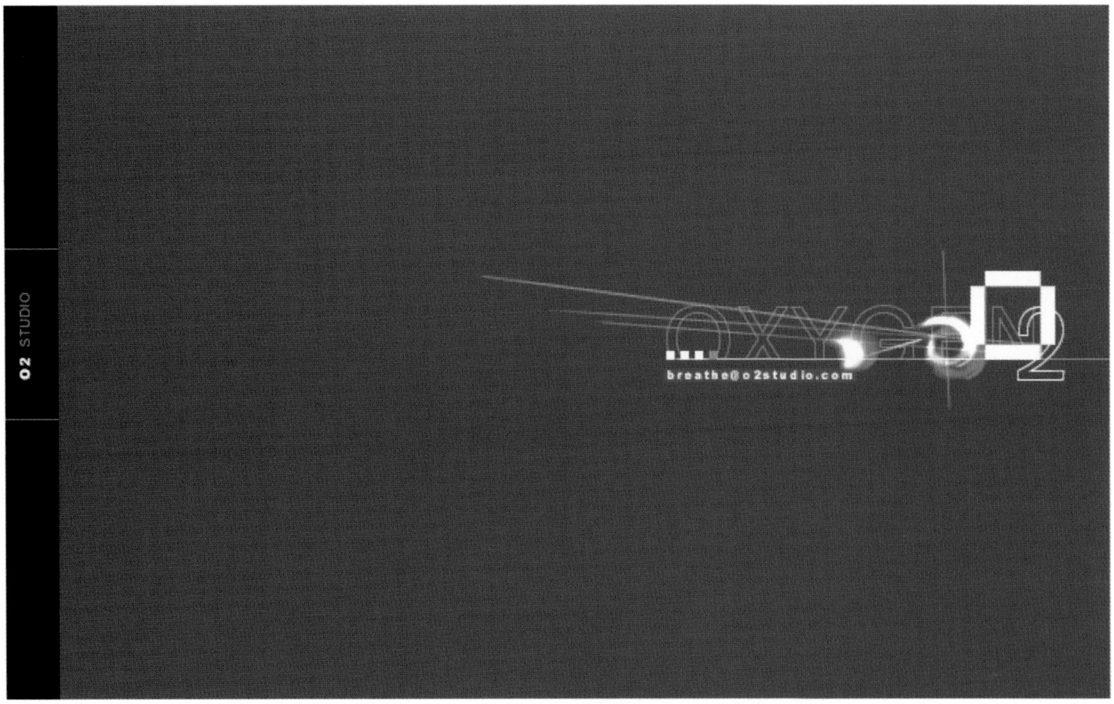

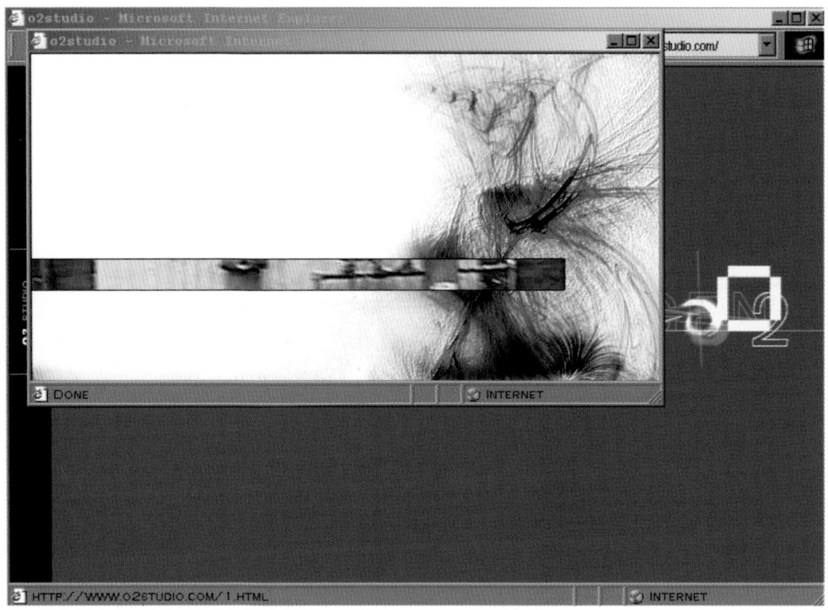

Title
o2 studios
URL
www.o2studios.com/
Design firm
o2 studios

The homepage of this site is clean and simple. The buttons don't give a hint as to their destinations and that underscores the point of the site.

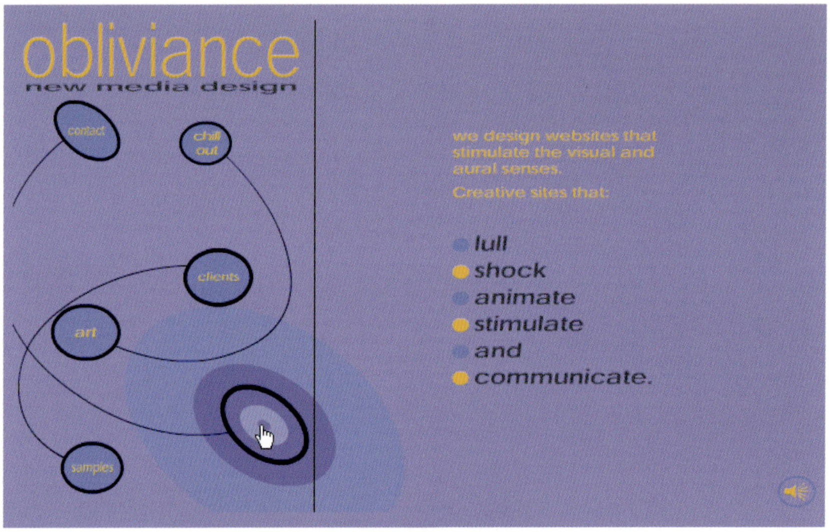

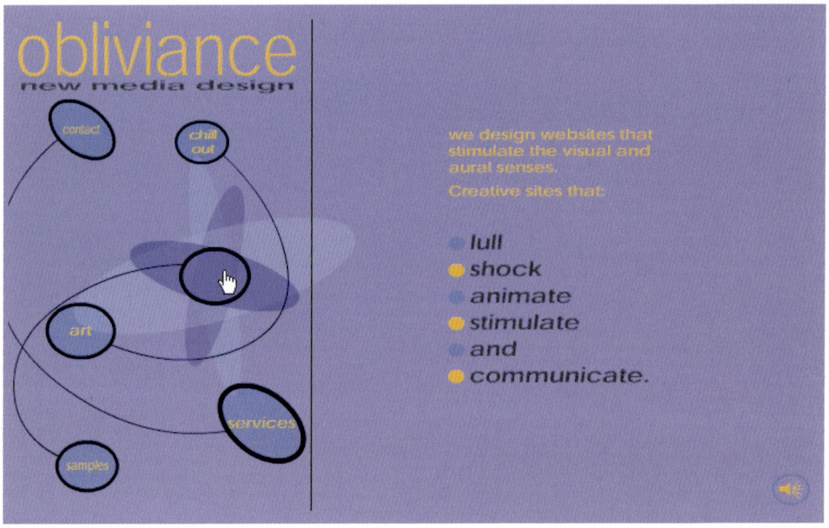

Title
obliviance
URL
obliviance.ndirect.co.uk/
Design firm
obliviance
Designer
Rosalind Miller

The Obliviance homepage is short and to the point. Six buttons and copy that succinctly describes what they do at that company—design Web sites that "stimulate the visual and aural senses."

Title
partyflights
URL
www.party-flights.com/
Design firm
party flights

Take a look at this busy homepage that works nonetheless. The Partyflights site is in constant movement and holds a bank of small buttons in the corner. The two windows scroll through images of Partyflight's various destinations.

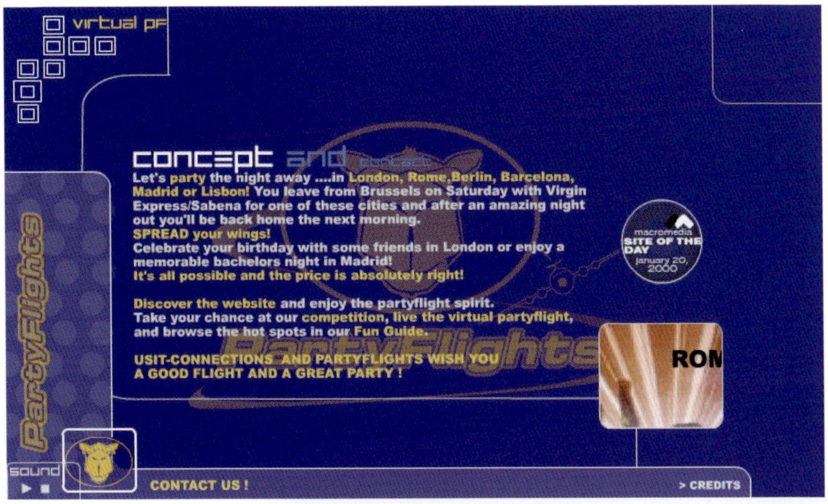

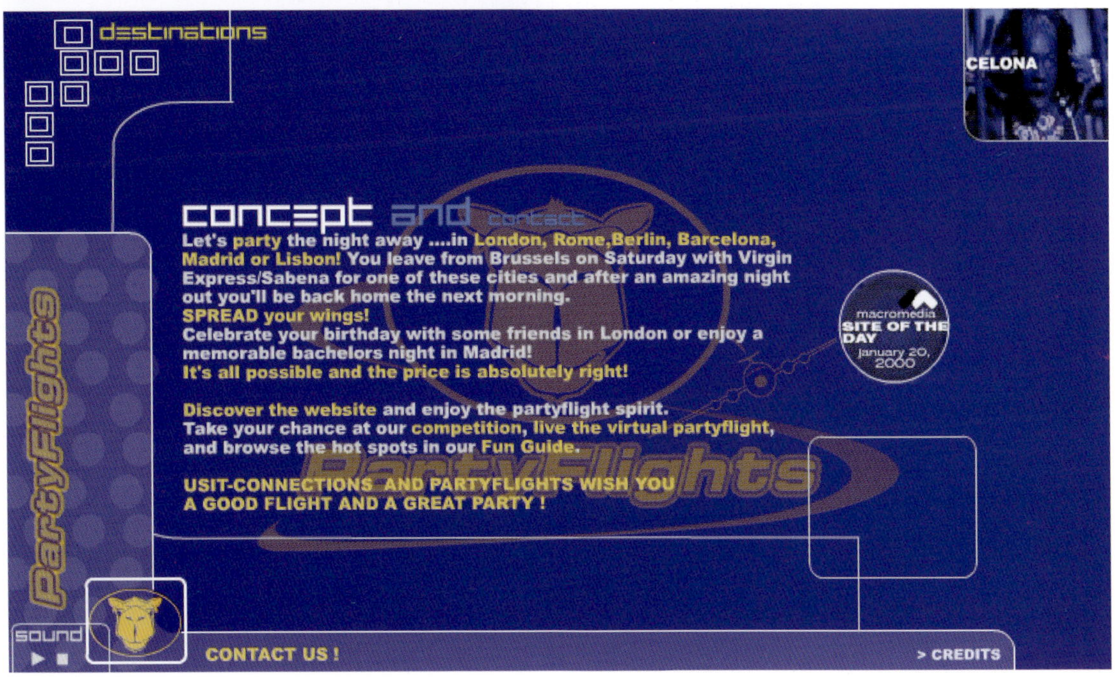

Title
ragingpixels
URL
www.ragingpixels.com/flash/ragingpixels.html
Design firm
Raging pixels

"Where art and technology merge." This homepage features a page that extends off the browser to the side. This is a nice change from the general trend of making sites that extend off the bottom of the browser.

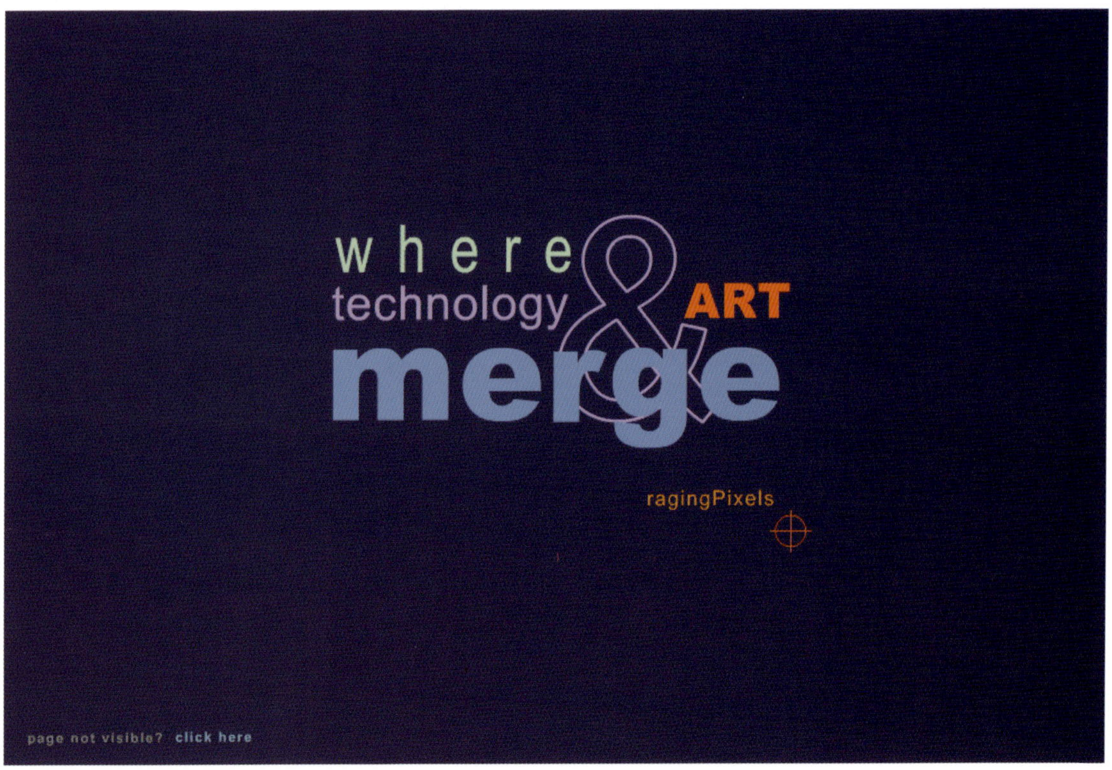

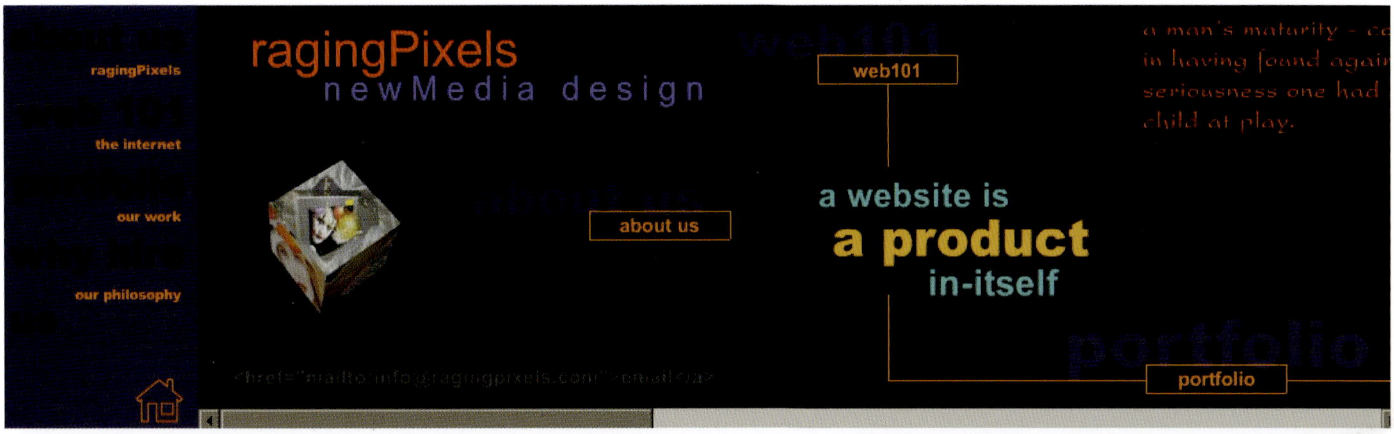
ragingPixels
the internet
our work
our philosophy
ragingPixels
newMedia design
web101
about us
a website is
a product
in-itself
portfolio
child at play.

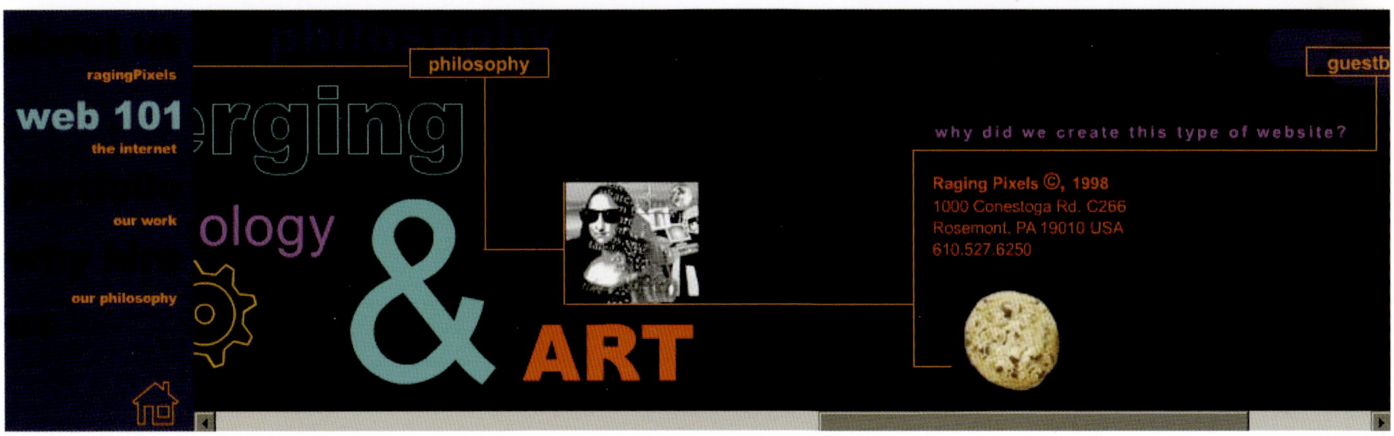
ragingPixels
web 101
the internet
our work
our philosophy
philosophy
ology
& ART
why did we create this type of website?
Raging Pixels ©, 1998
1000 Conestoga Rd. C266
Rosemont, PA 19010 USA
610.527.6250

Title
Resonant
URL
www.resonant.it/
Design firm
Resonant SRL

Resonant has a great little homepage that features a Flash pop-up window. The animation stars an "alien" that becomes the cursor over the navigation buttons.

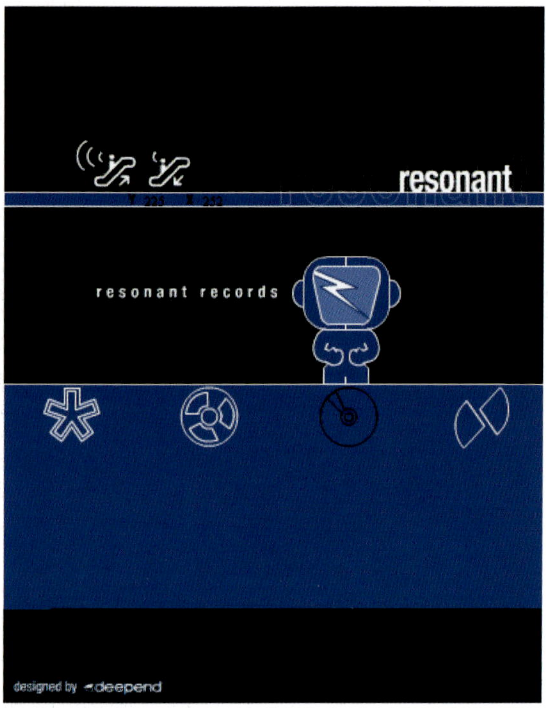

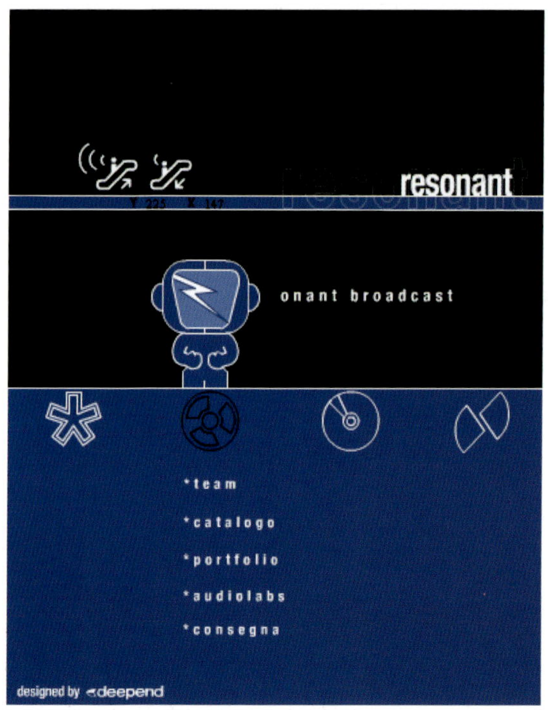

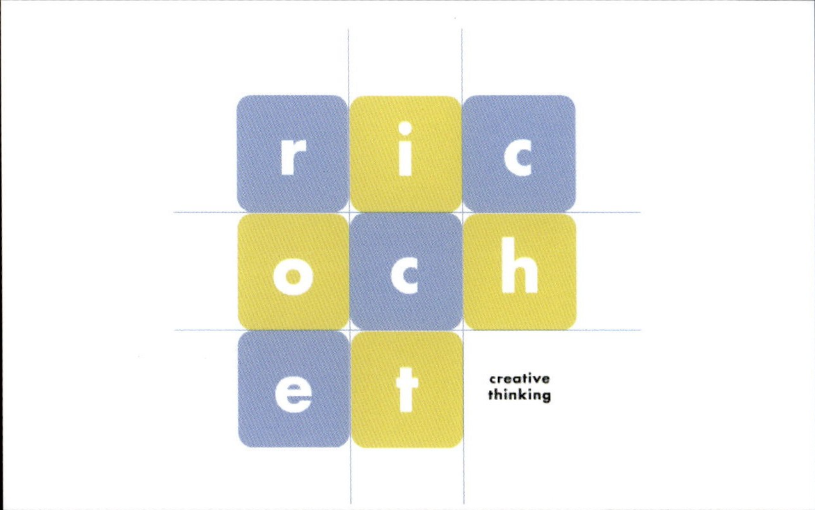
ric
och
et
creative
thinking

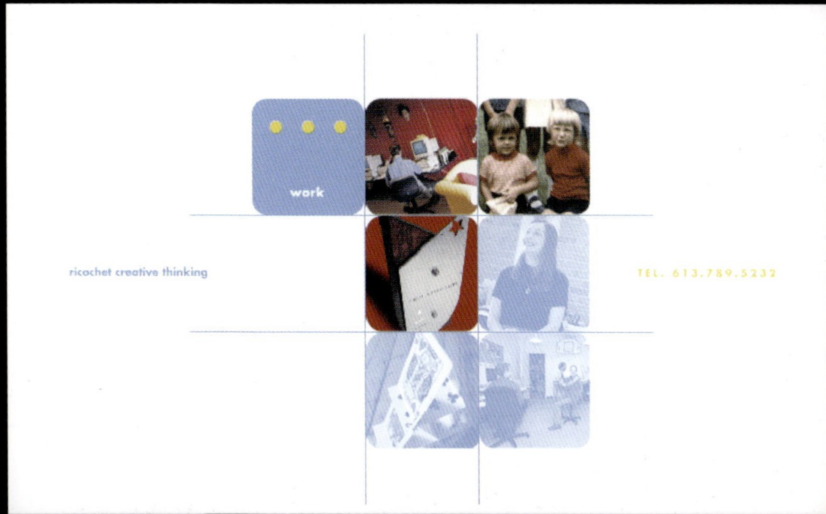
work
ricochet creative thinking
TEL. 613.789.5232

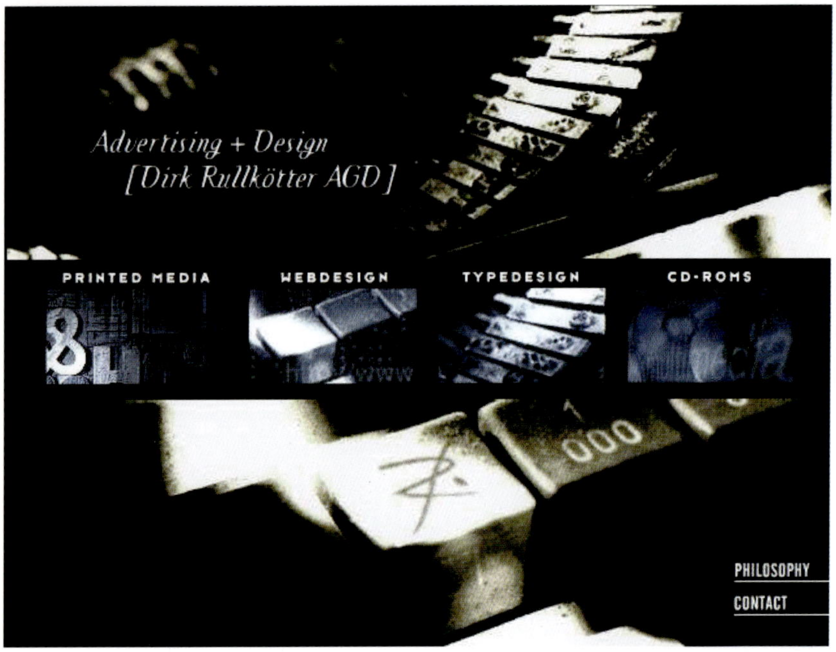

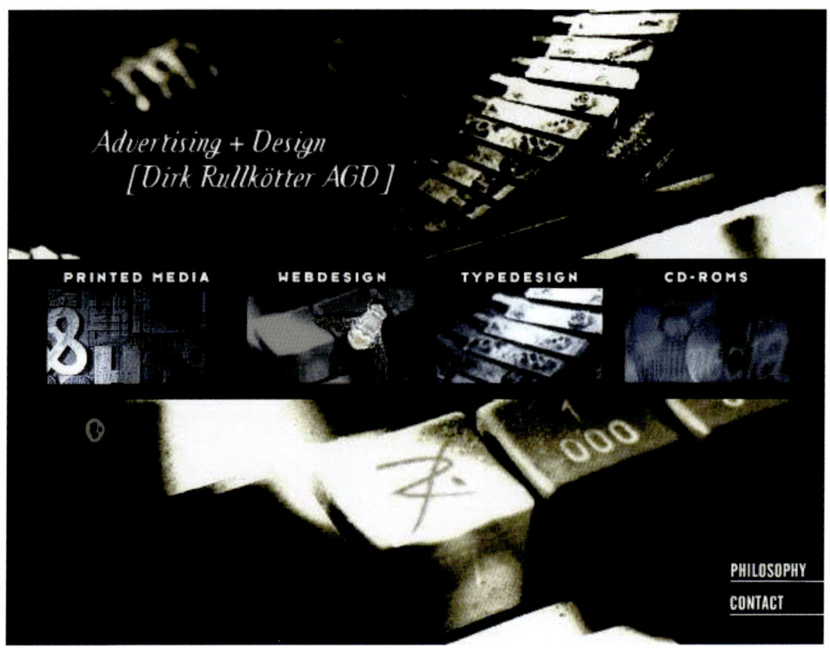

Title
Dirk Rullkötter
URL
www.rullkoetter.de/
Design firm
Rullkötter AGD Werbung + Design
Designer
Dirk Rullkötter

The main image of this splashpage is an interesting close-up photo. The real star of the homepage is a realistic bee that follows the cursor between the navigation buttons.

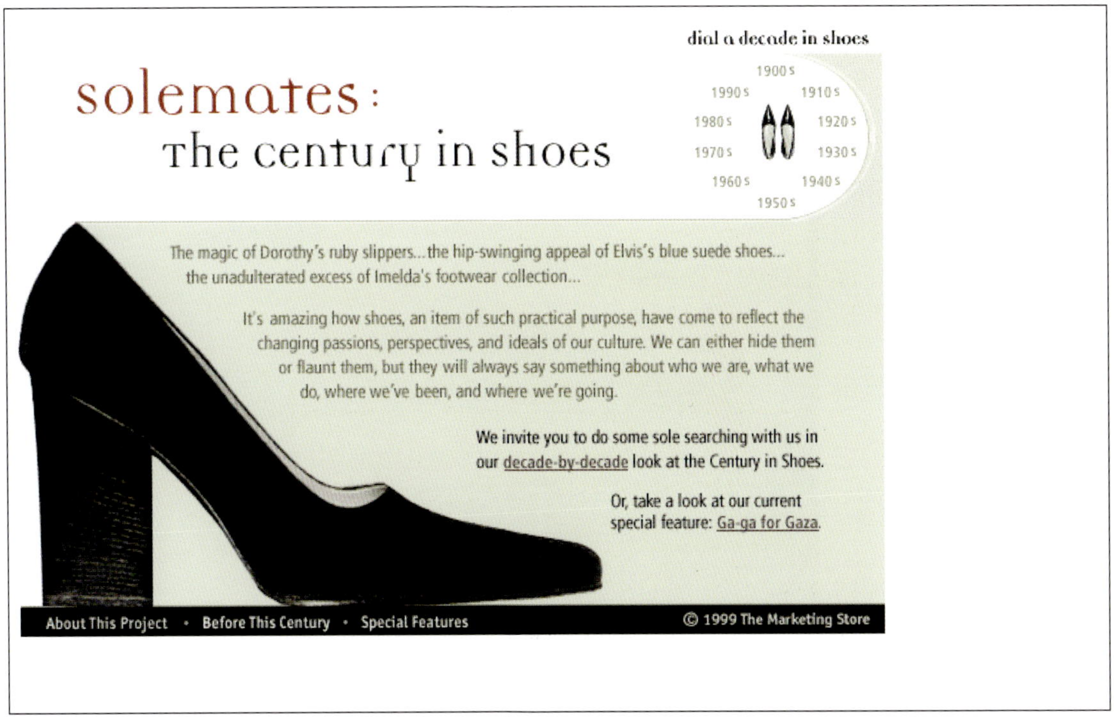

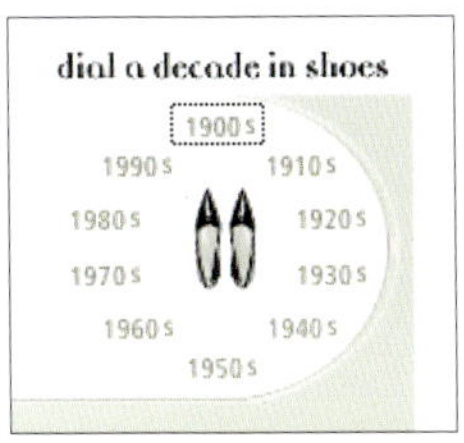

Title
solemates
URL
www.centuryinshoes.com/home.html
Design firm
The Marketing store

The unique "dial a decade" interface looks great juxtaposed against the large high-heeled shoe that dominates Solemates' design. Solemates also features excellent use of color.

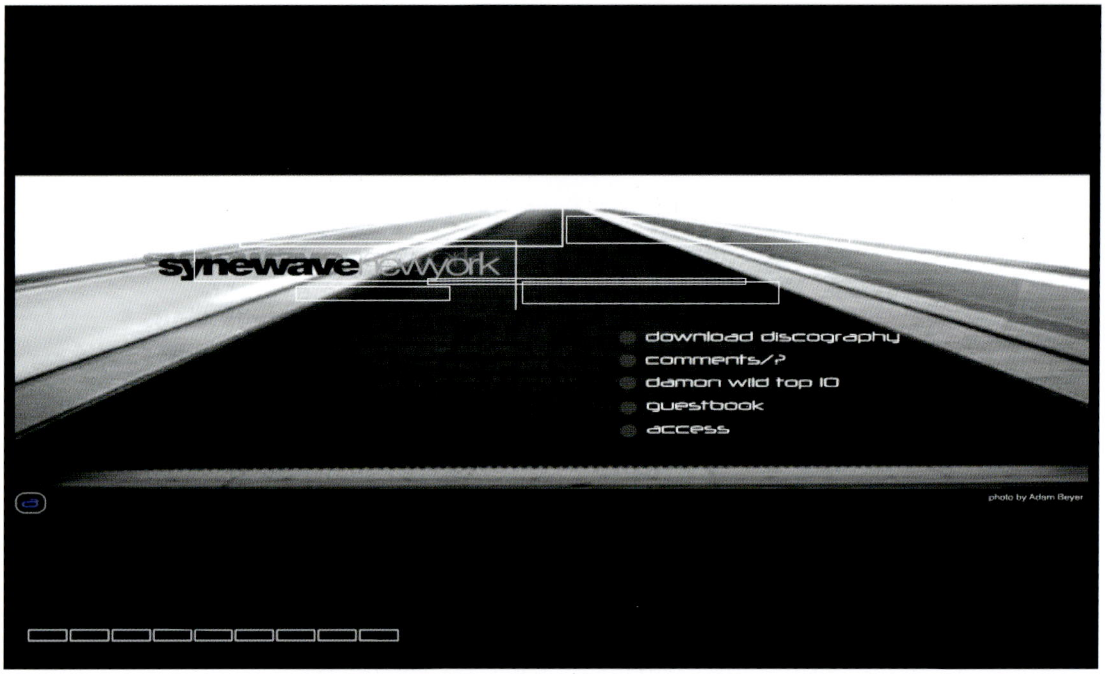

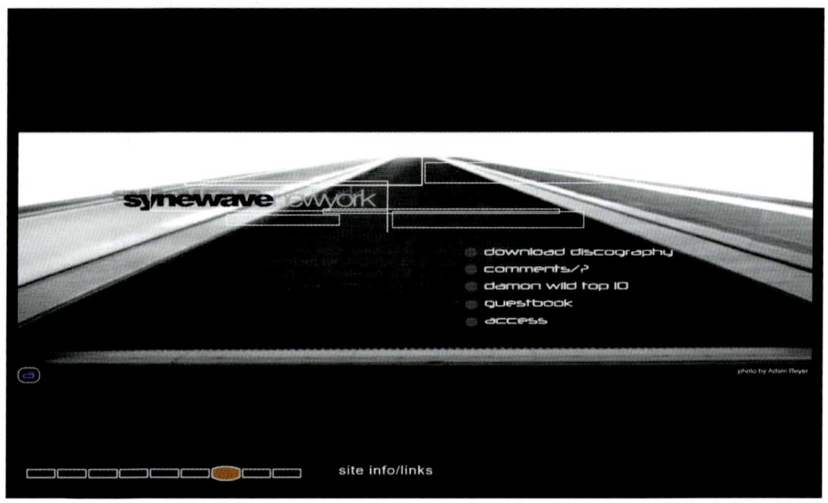

Title
synewave
URL
www.synewave.com/
Design firm
synewave
Designer
Damon wild

An unidentifiable photo is the primary image of this homepage. Almost like a road stretching off into the distance, this photo image conveys a sense of movement and excitement.

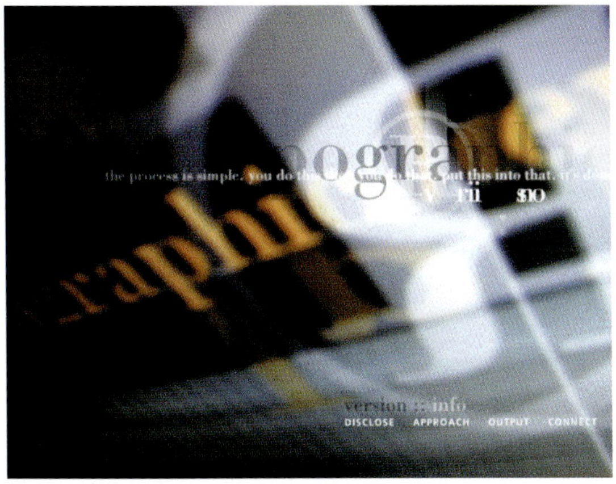

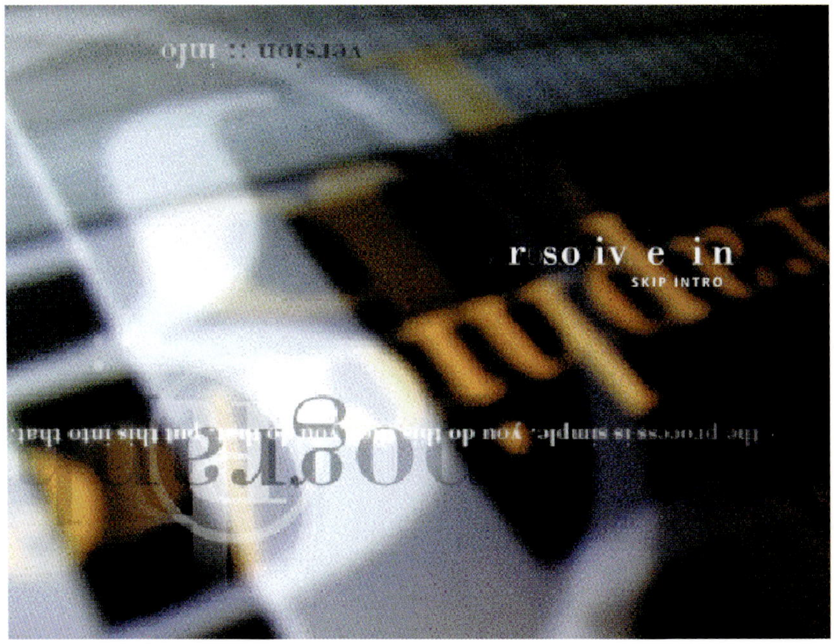

Title
Typographic
URL
www.typographic.com/
Design firm
Typographic
Designer
Jimmy Chen

Blurred and moving words dominate this site, which is appropriate for a company named Typographic. The buttons are very clear, drawing your attention away from the movement to make the site easy to navigate.

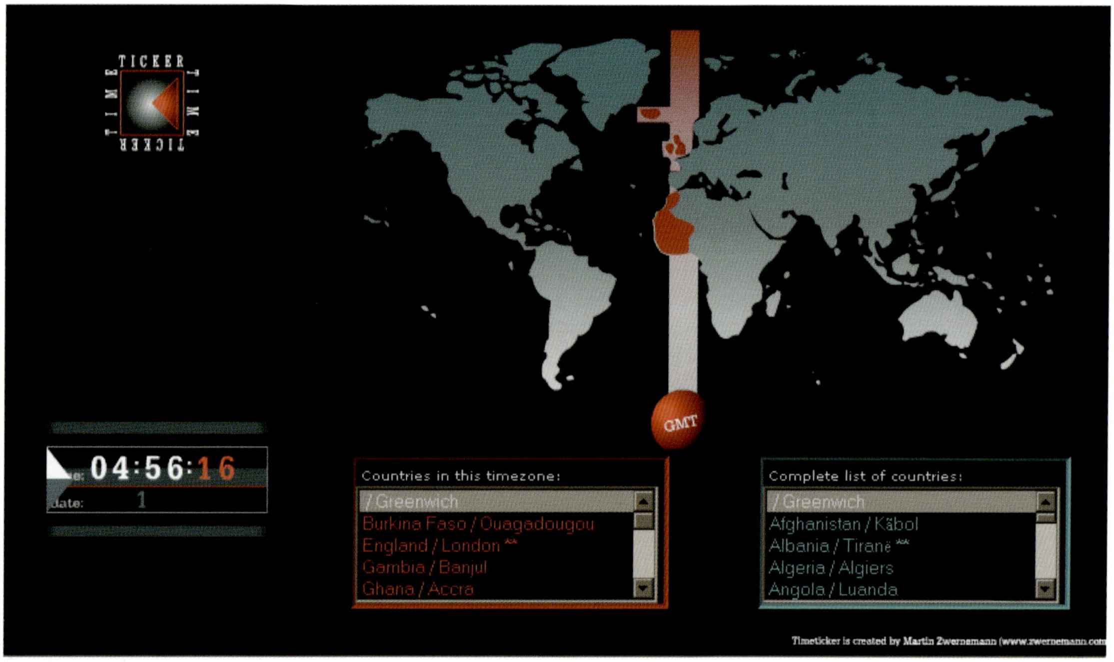

Title
Timeticker
URL
www.timeticker.com/
Design firm
zwernemann
Designer
Martin Zwernemann

The splashpage is the only page on this elegant site. The Flash-driven Web page tells you the time anywhere in the world. The various time zones are highlighted on mouse-over. Just click on a time zone to find out the time, down to the second, wherever you are.

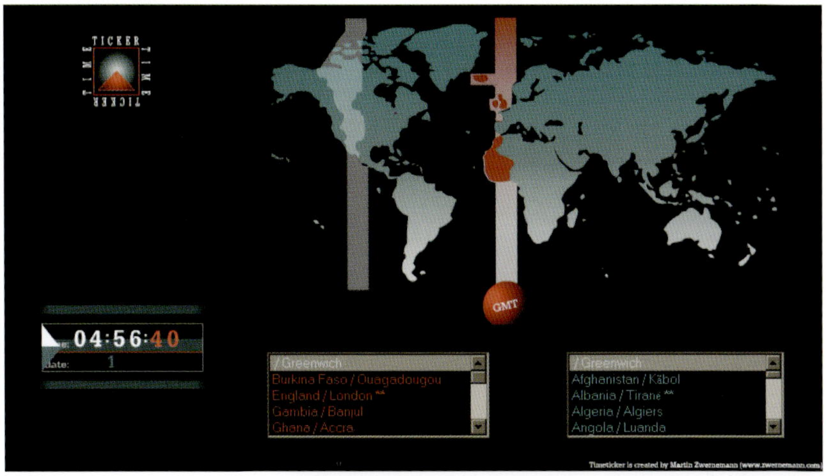
GMT
04:56:40
date: 1
/ Greenwich
Burkina Faso / Ouagadougou
England / London **
Gambia / Banjul
Ghana / Accra
/ Greenwich
Afghanistan / Kābol
Albania / Tirane **
Algeria / Algiers
Angola / Luanda
Timeticker is created by Martin Zwernemann (www.zwernemann.com)

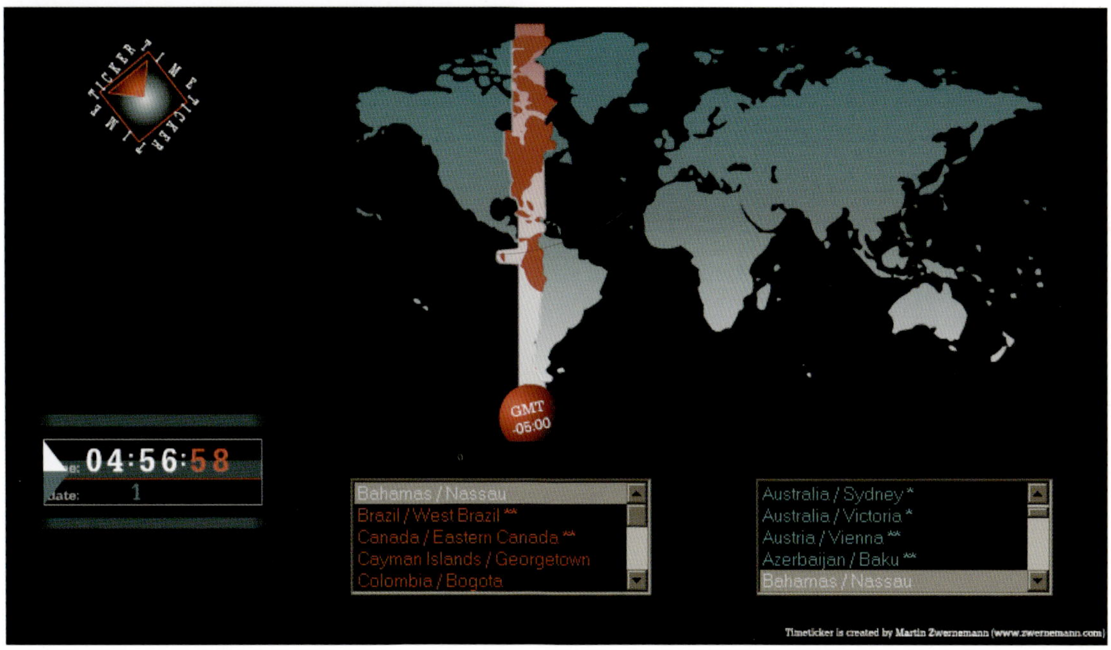
GMT
-05:00
04:56:58
date: 1
Bahamas / Nassau
Brazil / West Brazil **
Canada / Eastern Canada **
Cayman Islands / Georgetown
Colombia / Bogota
Australia / Sydney *
Australia / Victoria *
Austria / Vienna **
Azerbaijan / Baku **
Bahamas / Nassau
Timeticker is created by Martin Zwernemann (www.zwernemann.com)

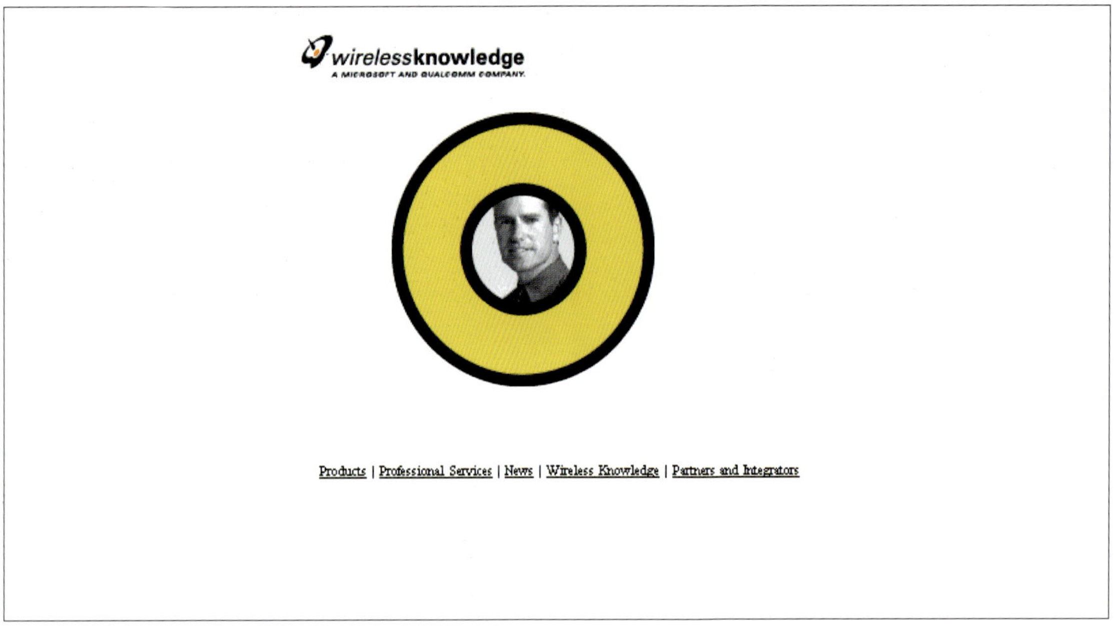

Title
wireless Knowledge
URL
www.wirelessknowledge.com/
Design firm
wireless Knowledge LLC

The Wireless Knowledge homepage is one simple interface with three buttons making a circle. They employ photos of people using their product to fill the circle.

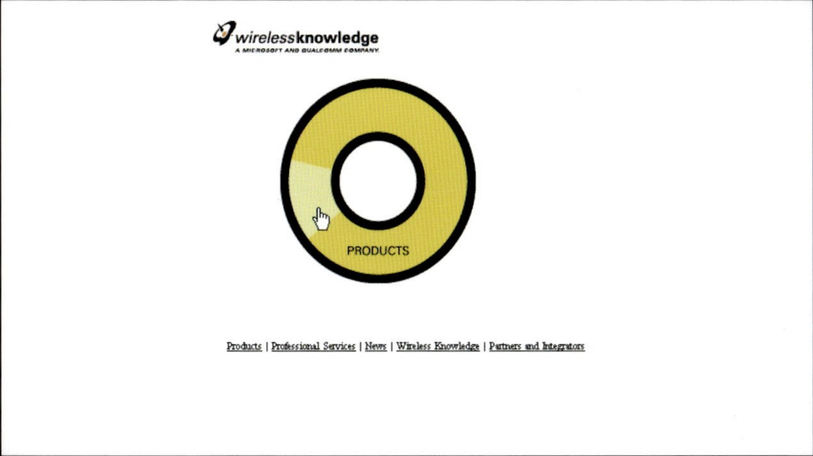
wirelessknowledge
A MICROSOFT AND QUALCOMM COMPANY.
PRODUCTS
Products | Professional Services | News | Wireless Knowledge | Partners and Integrators

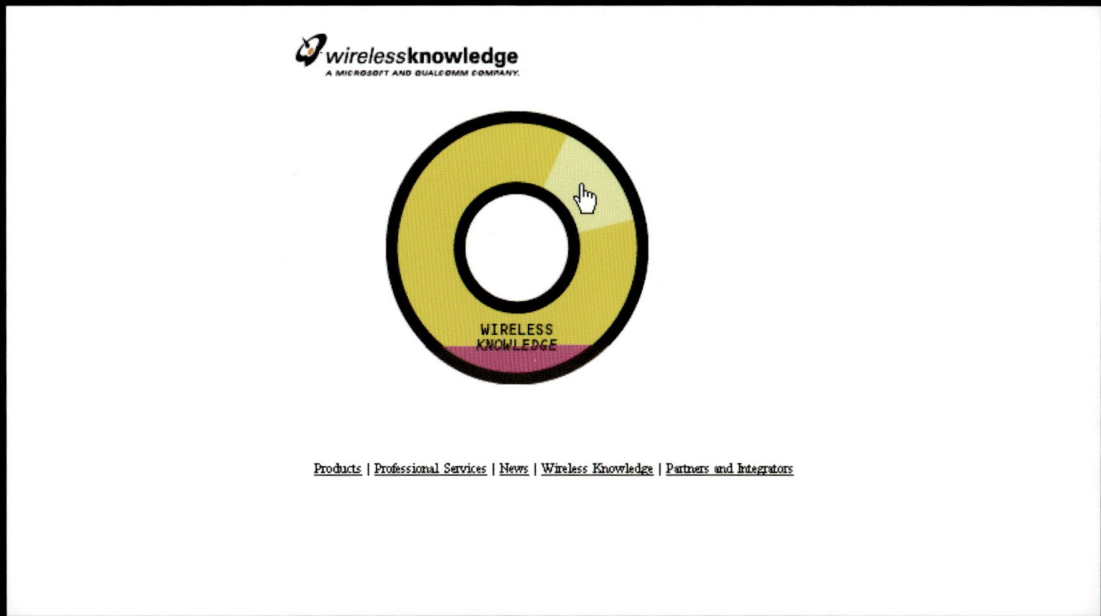
wirelessknowledge
A MICROSOFT AND QUALCOMM COMPANY.
WIRELESS
KNOWLEDGE
Products | Professional Services | News | Wireless Knowledge | Partners and Integrators

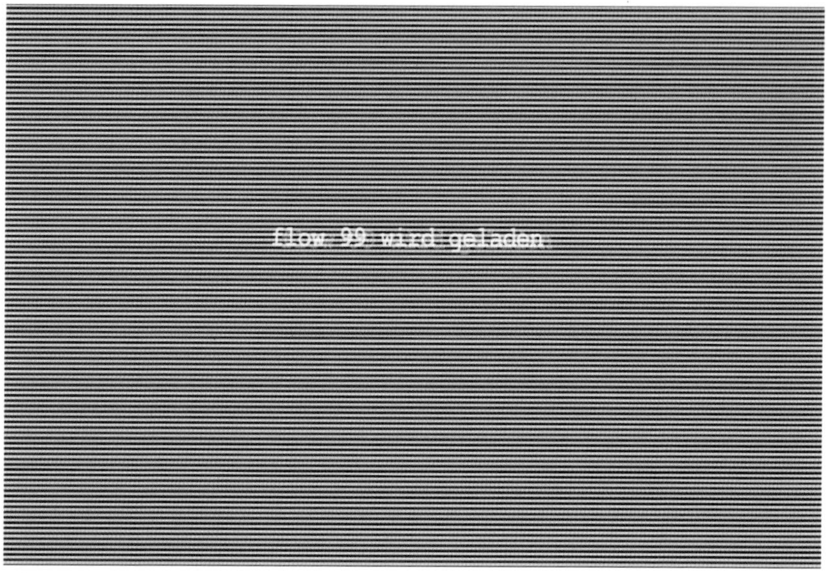

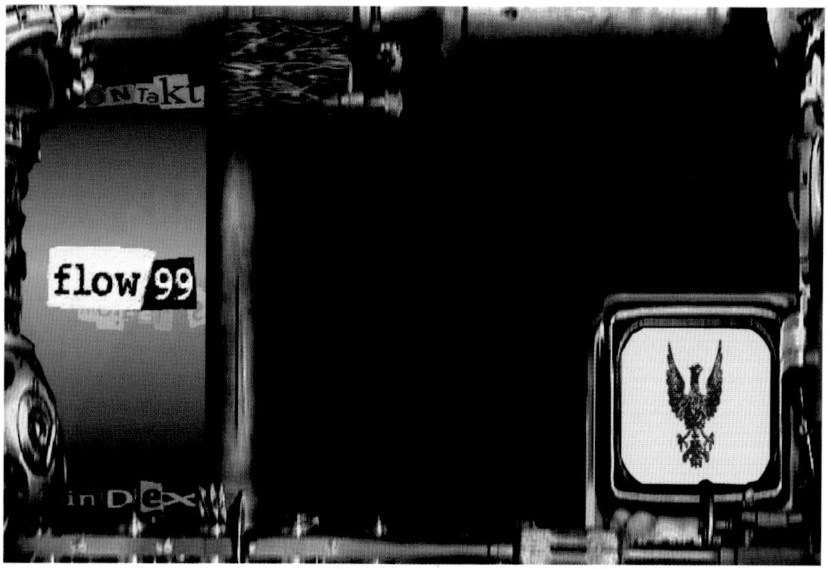

Title
wojtek
URL
www.wojtek.de/
Design Firm
perplex GMBH
Designer
sal wojtek

This homepage creates an otherworldly atmosphere that carries over into the rest of the site. The navigation bar down the side of the page scrolls by on mouse-over and has cool sound associated with it.

Title
planet p-o-d
URL
www.p-o-d.co.uk/
Design Firm
pod New Media Ltd.

The p-o-d homepage features their odd assortment of aliens and spaceships for you to meet. The piano music in the background is great and a refreshing change from the standard techno beat.

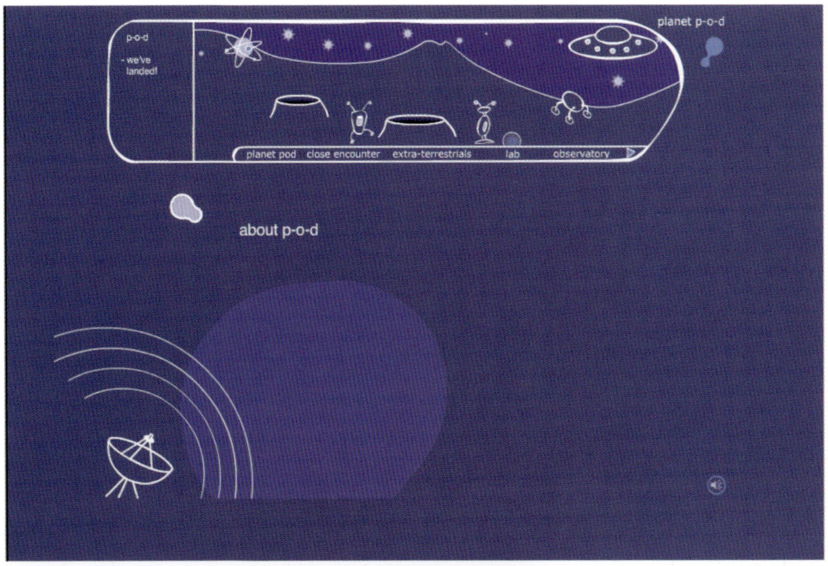

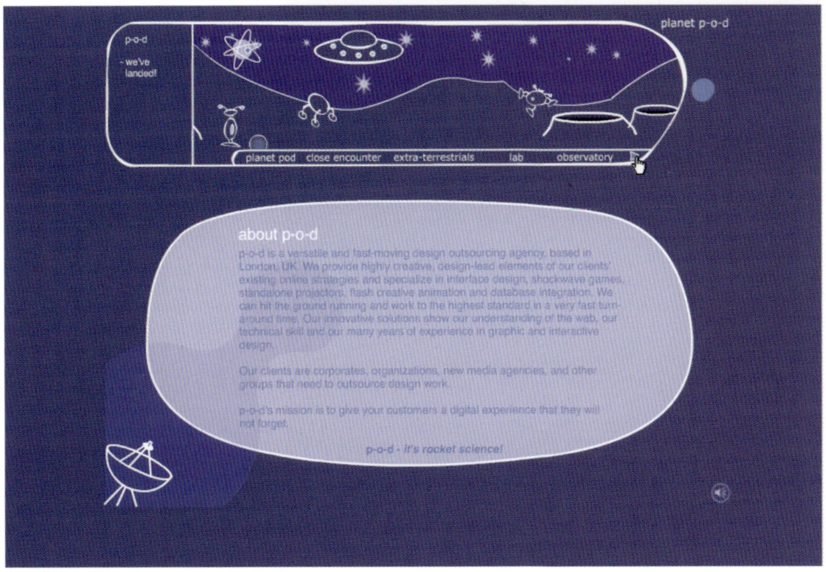

Title
online interview with Randall Larson
URL
people.mn.mediaone.net/gonzoz
Design Firm
online interview with Randall Larson

Randall Larson's homepage is a work of Web-design art. Everything on this page is a button that lights up on mouse-over and tells you what it reveals. Stars follow the cursor around the screen but they can be turned off if you prefer.

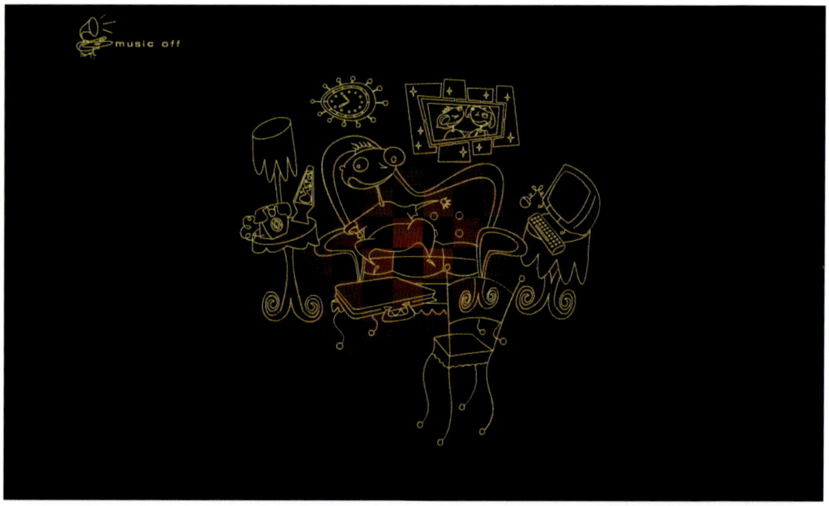

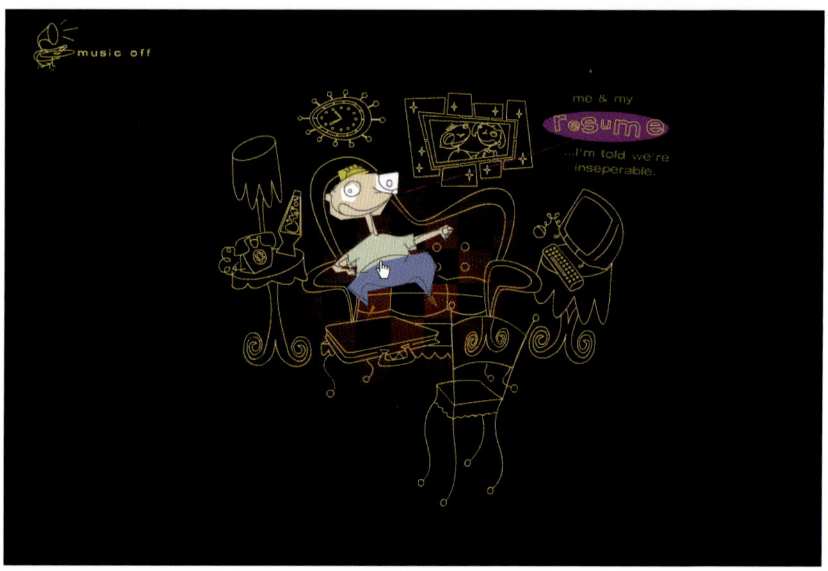

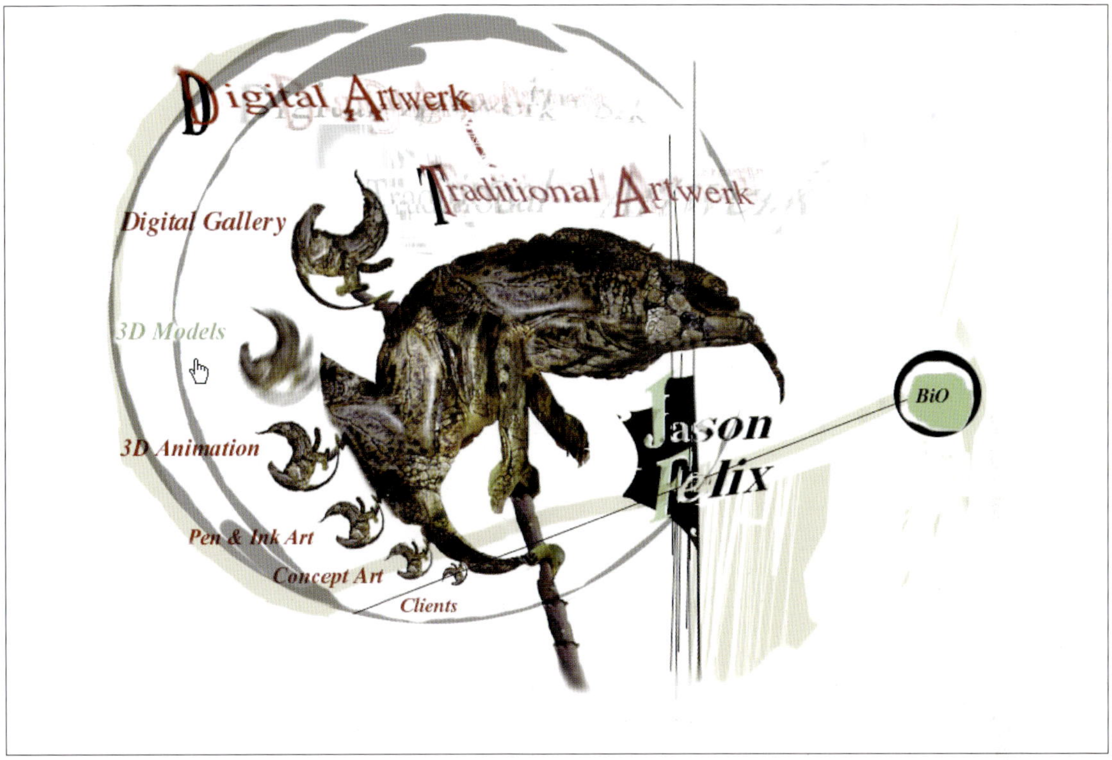

Title
Jason Felix
URL
www.jasonfelix.com/newinterface.html
Design Firm
Jason Felix
Designer
Jason Felix

This personal homepage features a single repeated image. This HTML site shows that great design does not need Flash or other animation programs to be great.

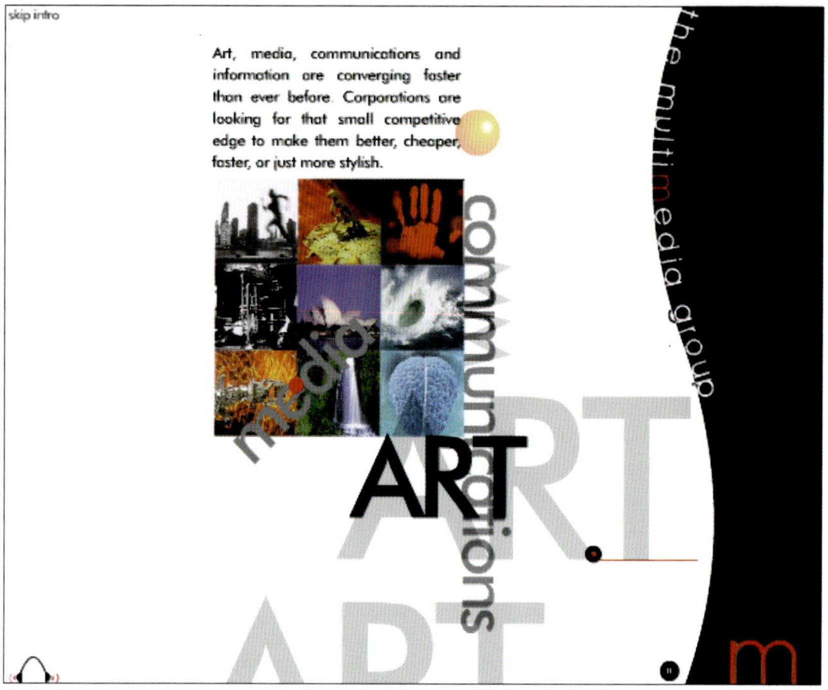

Title
The Multimedia Group
URL
www.themmgroup.com/
Design Firm
The Multimedia Group

Art, commerce, and design come together on the Multimedia Group's Web site. A lot of Flash movement enhances the various buttons on the homepage.

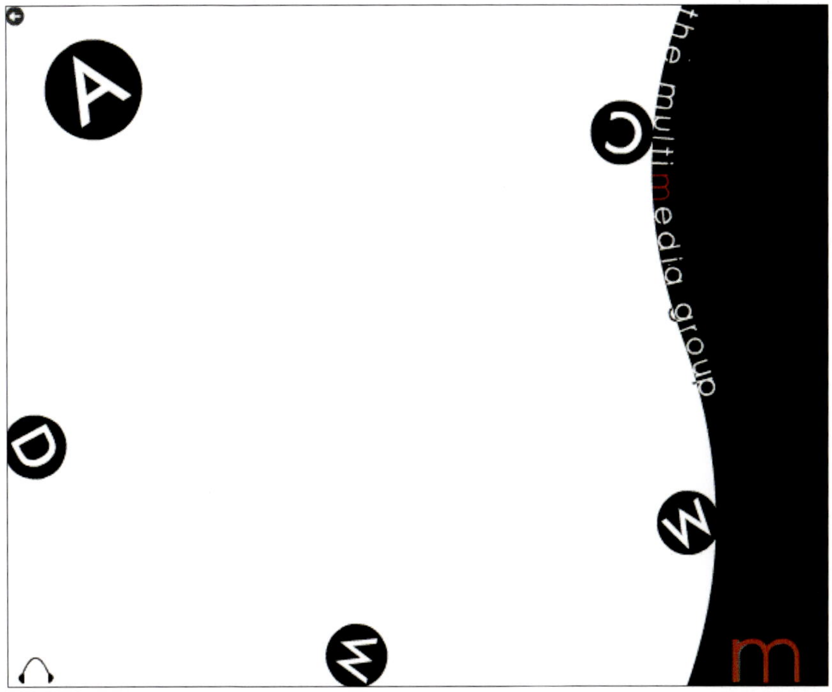
the multimedia group
m

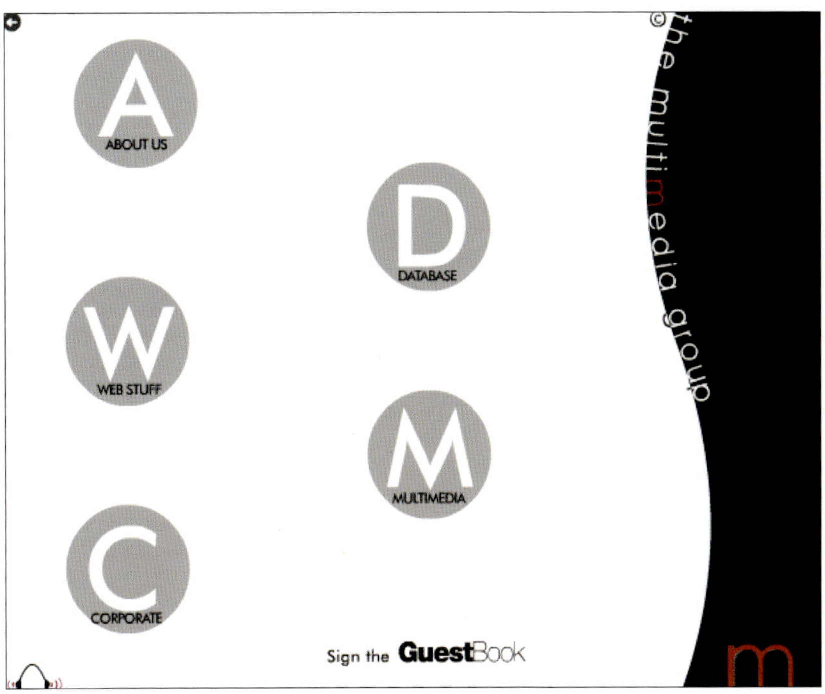
©
the multimedia group
ABOUT US
DATABASE
WEB STUFF
MULTIMEDIA
CORPORATE
Sign the GuestBook
m

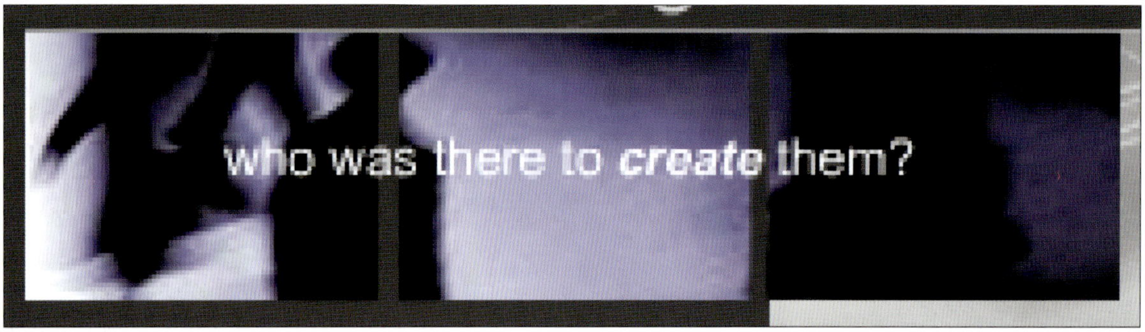

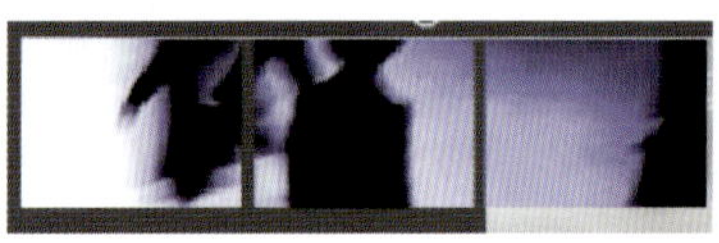

Title
Envision Interactive
URL
www.envisioninteractive.com/
Design Firm
Envision Interactive

The Envision splashpage has a single image behind three frames that dances around to create motion. Flash keeps bandwidth to a minimum.

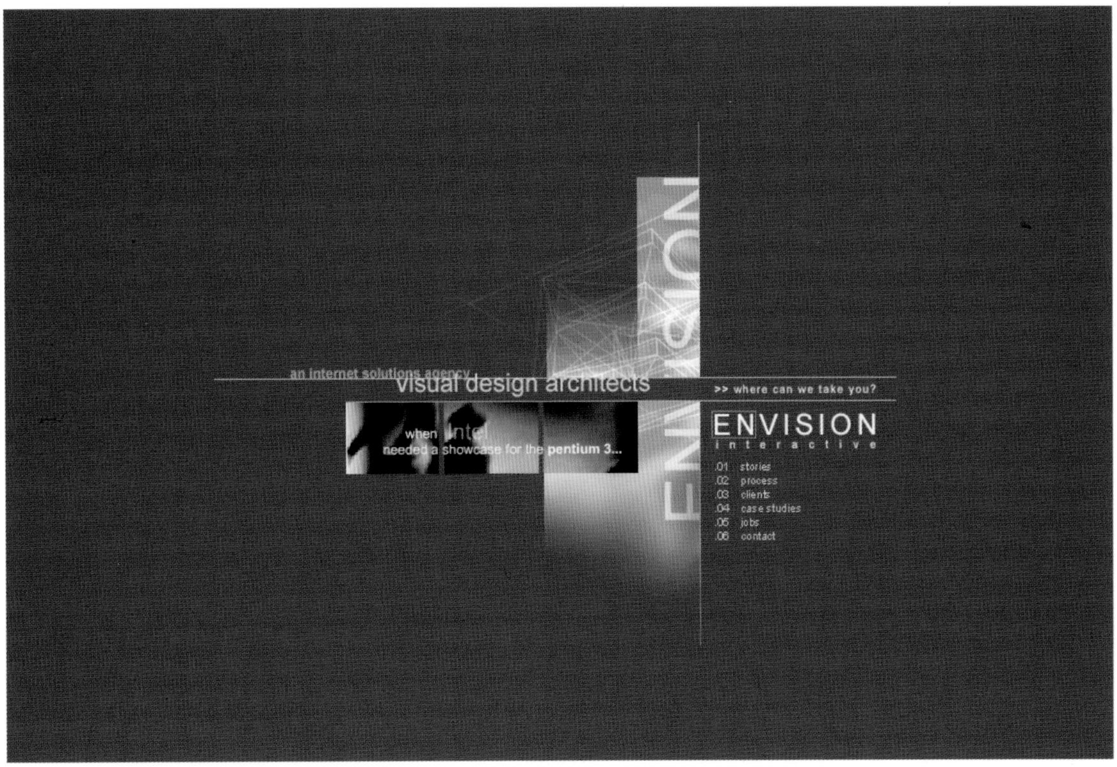
an internet solutions agency
visual design architects
>> where can we take you?
when intel
needed a showcase for the pentium 3...
ENVISION
interactive
.01 stories
.02 process
.03 clients
.04 case studies
.05 jobs
.06 contact
ENVISION

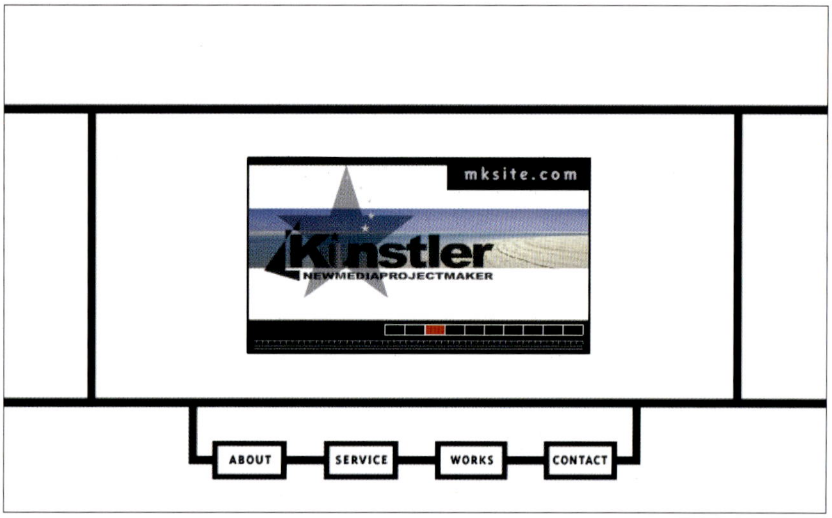
mksite.com
Künstler
NEWMEDIAPROJECTMAKER
ABOUT
SERVICE
WORKS
CONTACT

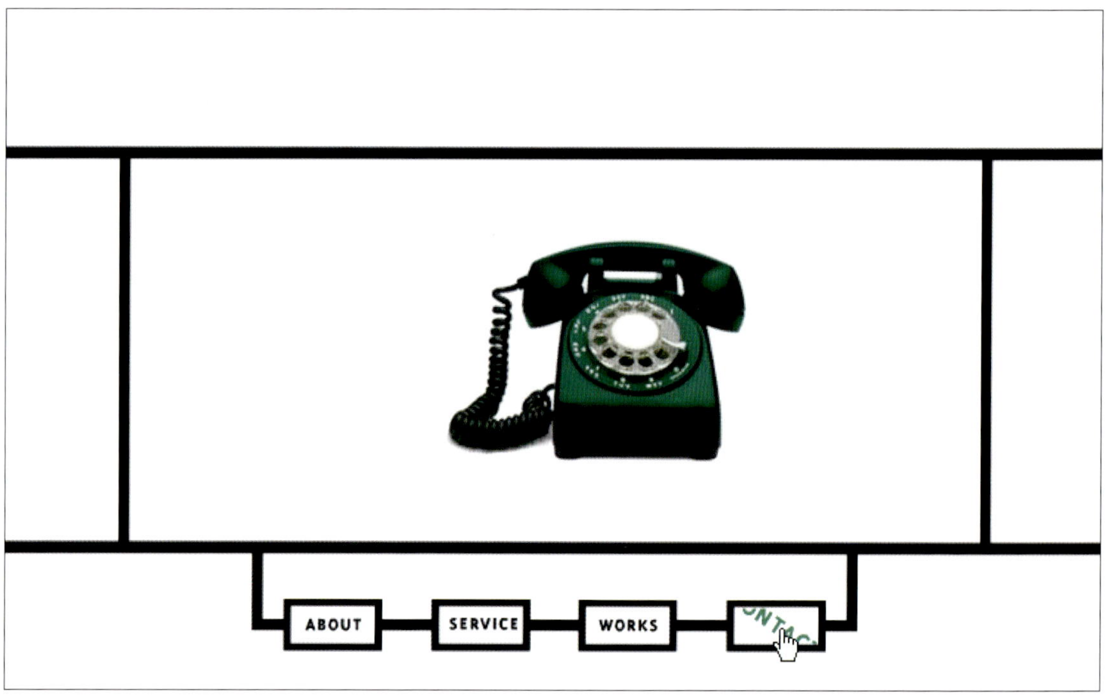
ABOUT
SERVICE
WORKS

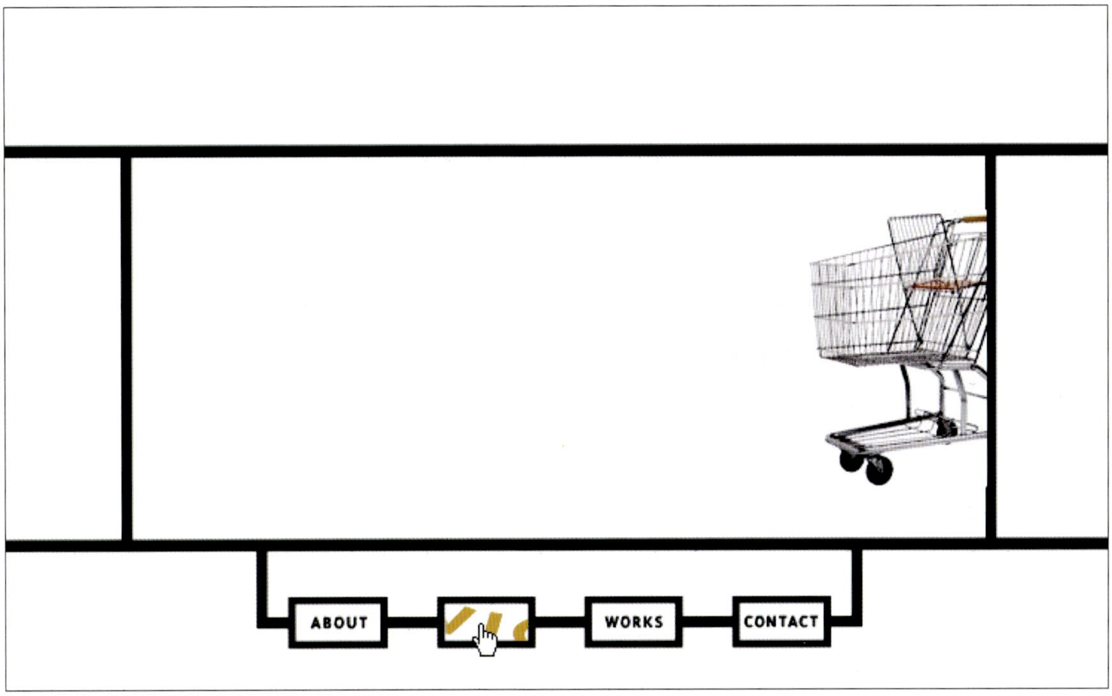

Title
MKsite
URL
mksite.com/
Design firm
MKsite
Designer
Massimo Kunstler

The MKSite homepage uses Flash to create an interface with iconic images that slide into the center window. The images on this site are amazingly sharp.

Title
Eurorunner
URL
www.eurorunner.com/
Design Firm
Euro.runner srl
Designers
Jacopo Deyla/Flash, Guiseppe Covino/Art Director, Franco Milazzo/Technical

Eurorunner uses to Macromedia's Flash to create a blowtorch effect that burns the e logo into the screen. The four bars slide onto the screen and frame the buttons.

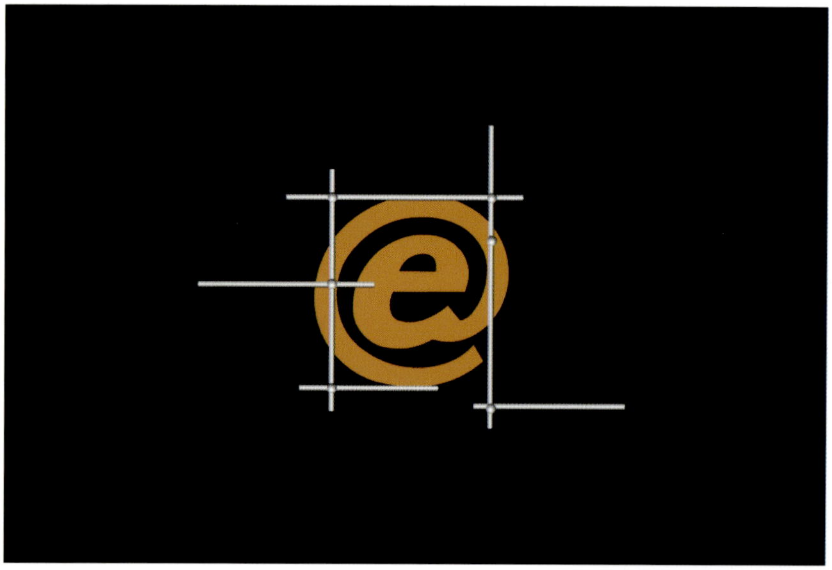

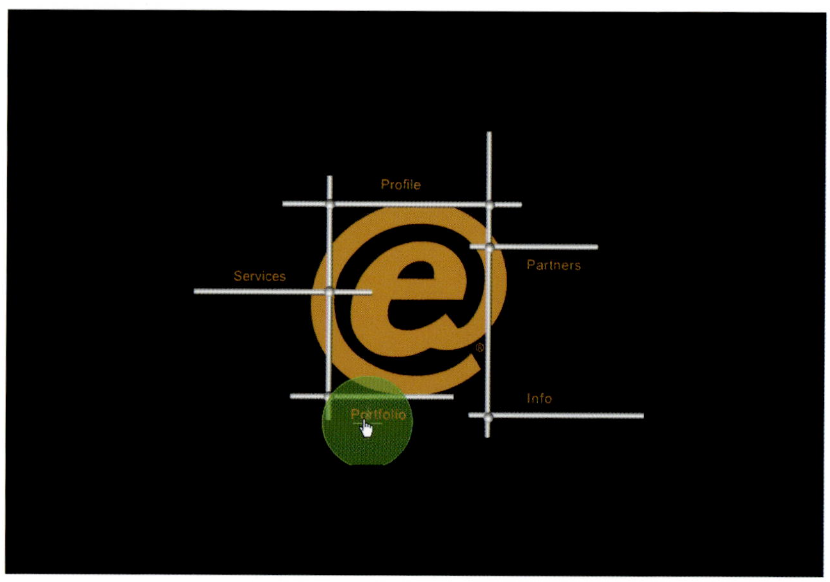

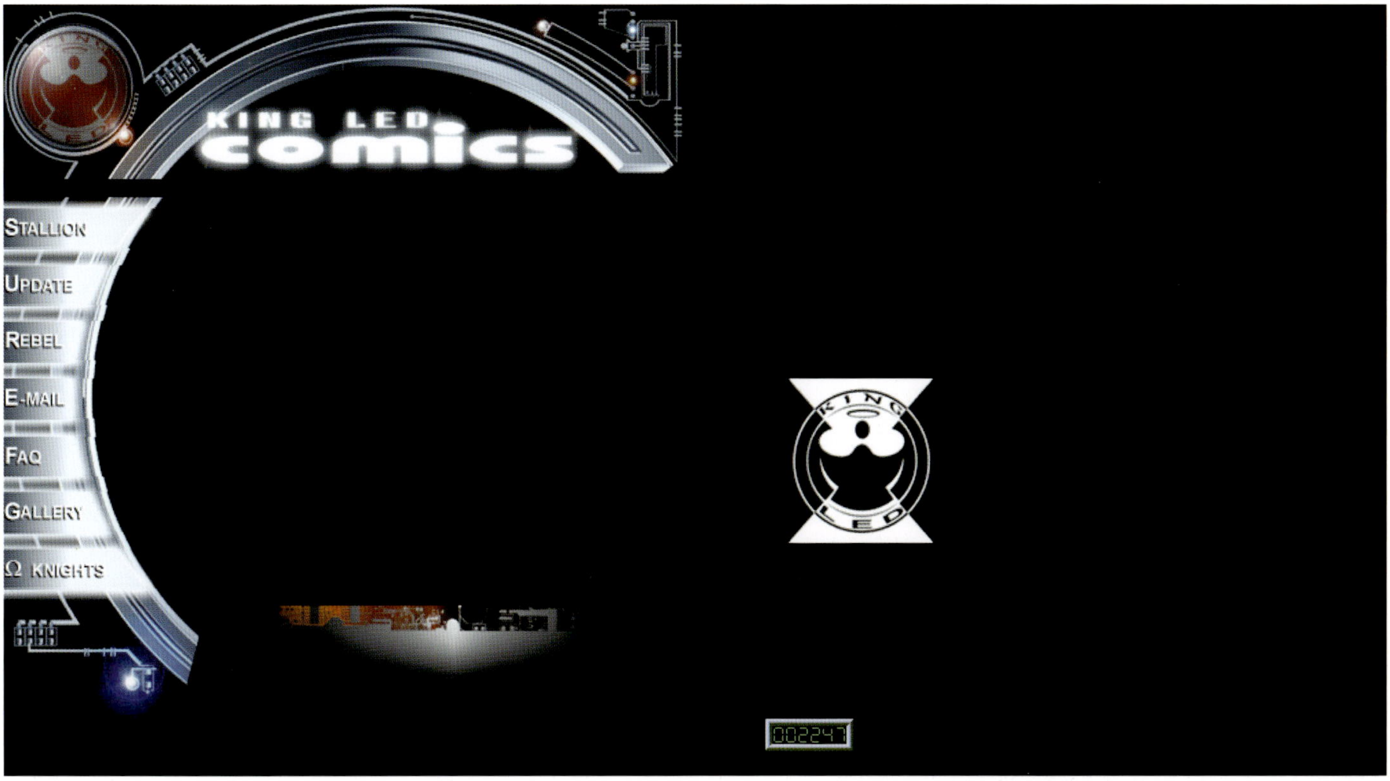

Title
King Led comics
URL
www3.sympatico.ca/kingled/
Design firm
King Led comics
Designer
Louis Douzepis

The use of extremely lush .jpeg images and a black background make a very pretty site. The homepage interface works as a frame that borders the rest of the images.

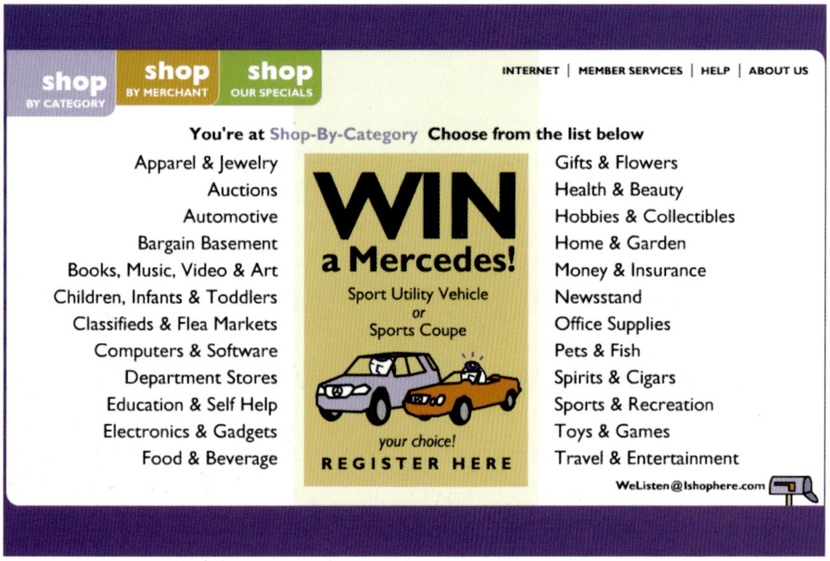
shop BY CATEGORY
shop BY MERCHANT
shop OUR SPECIALS
INTERNET | MEMBER SERVICES | HELP | ABOUT US
You're at Shop-By-Category Choose from the list below
Apparel & Jewelry
Auctions
Automotive
Bargain Basement
Books, Music, Video & Art
Children, Infants & Toddlers
Classifieds & Flea Markets
Computers & Software
Department Stores
Education & Self Help
Electronics & Gadgets
Food & Beverage
WIN
a Mercedes!
Sport Utility Vehicle
or
Sports Coupe
your choice!
REGISTER HERE
Gifts & Flowers
Health & Beauty
Hobbies & Collectibles
Home & Garden
Money & Insurance
Newsstand
Office Supplies
Pets & Fish
Spirits & Cigars
Sports & Recreation
Toys & Games
Travel & Entertainment
WeListen@Ishophere.com

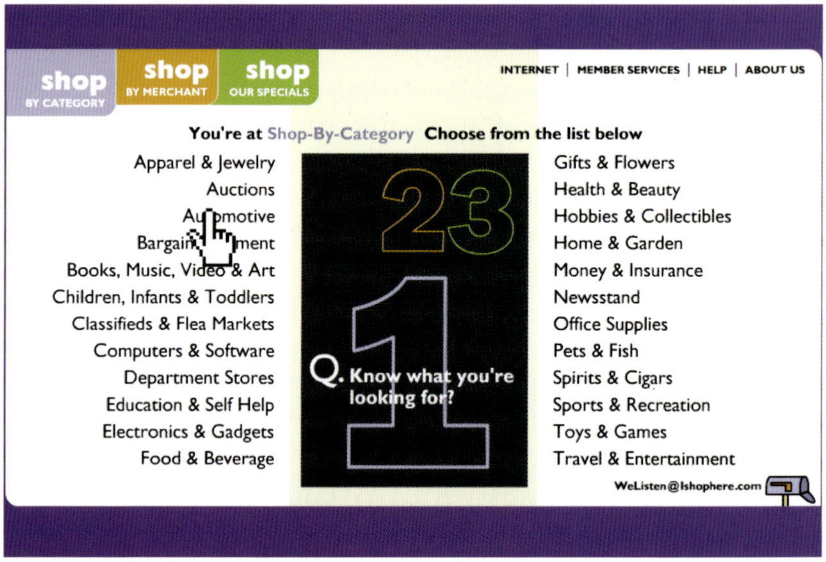
shop BY CATEGORY
shop BY MERCHANT
shop OUR SPECIALS
INTERNET | MEMBER SERVICES | HELP | ABOUT US
You're at Shop-By-Category Choose from the list below
Apparel & Jewelry
Auctions
Children, Infants & Toddlers
Classifieds & Flea Markets
Computers & Software
Department Stores
Education & Self Help
Electronics & Gadgets
Food & Beverage
23
1
Gifts & Flowers
Health & Beauty
Hobbies & Collectibles
Home & Garden
Money & Insurance
Newsstand
Office Supplies
Pets & Fish
Spirits & Cigars
Sports & Recreation
Toys & Games
Travel & Entertainment
WeListen@Ishophere.com

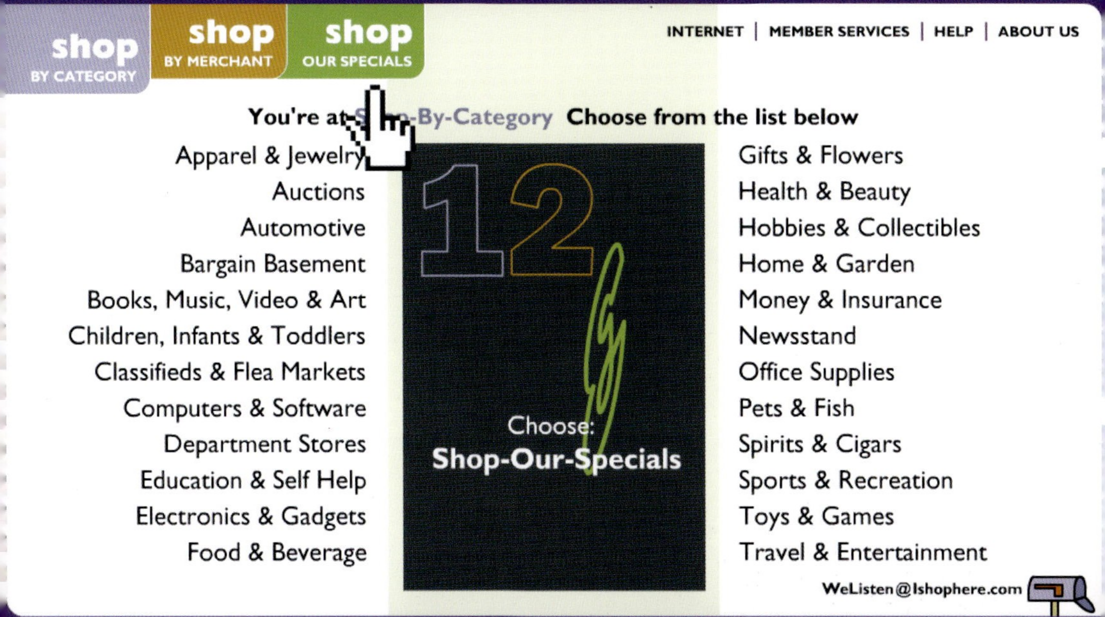
shop
BY CATEGORY
shop
BY MERCHANT
shop
OUR SPECIALS
INTERNET | MEMBER SERVICES | HELP | ABOUT US
You're at -By-Category Choose from the list below
Apparel & Jewelry
Auctions
Automotive
Bargain Basement
Books, Music, Video & Art
Children, Infants & Toddlers
Classifieds & Flea Markets
Computers & Software
Department Stores
Education & Self Help
Electronics & Gadgets
Food & Beverage
12
Choose:
Shop-Our-Specials
Gifts & Flowers
Health & Beauty
Hobbies & Collectibles
Home & Garden
Money & Insurance
Newsstand
Office Supplies
Pets & Fish
Spirits & Cigars
Sports & Recreation
Toys & Games
Travel & Entertainment
WeListen@Ishophere.com

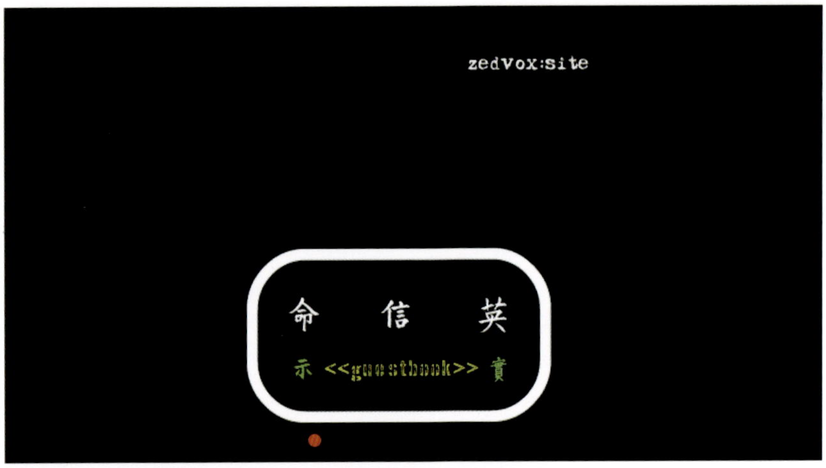

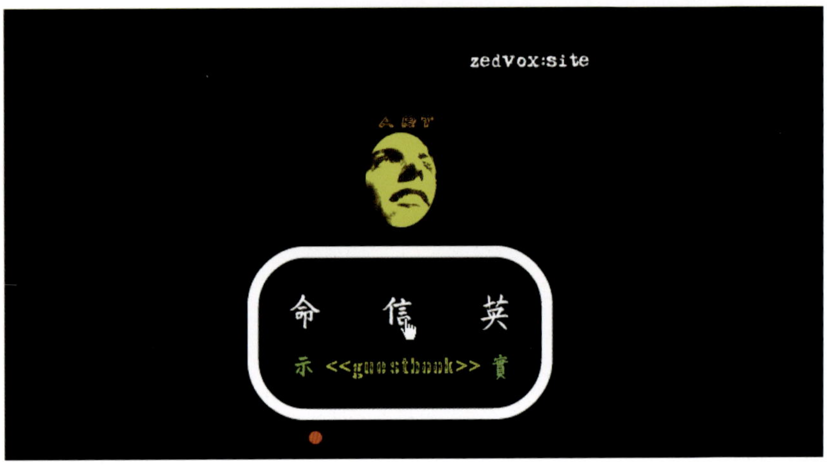

Title
zedmain
URL
www.members.tripod.com/zedvox/zedmain.html
Design firm
zedmain

This homepage has a very simple, black background with three excellent buttons that light up different areas on mouse-over.

Title
clint Baker's portfolio viewing Machine
URL
www.clintbaker.com/
Design firm
clint Baker

See the "Amazing Picture Viewer!" Look at a great splashpage that has a historical theme. The single button on top displays a different thumbnail on each mouse-over. Click on an image to see the full screen.

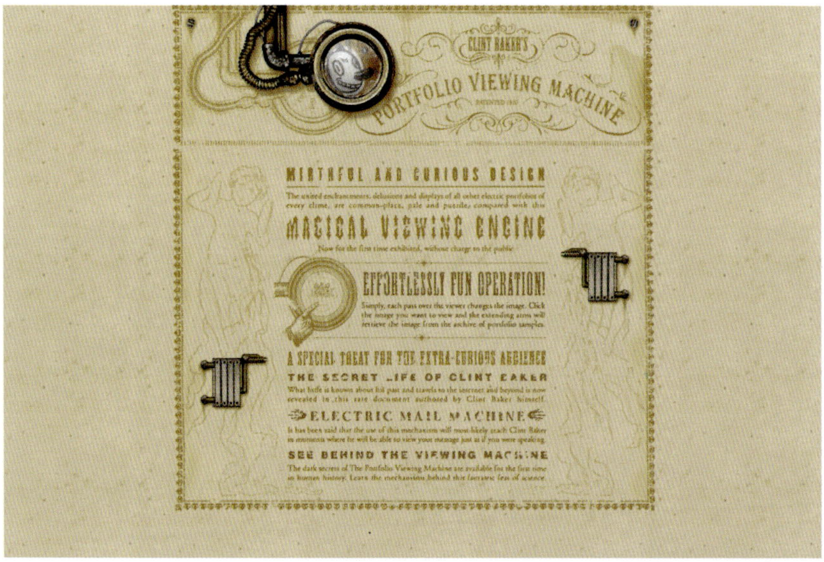

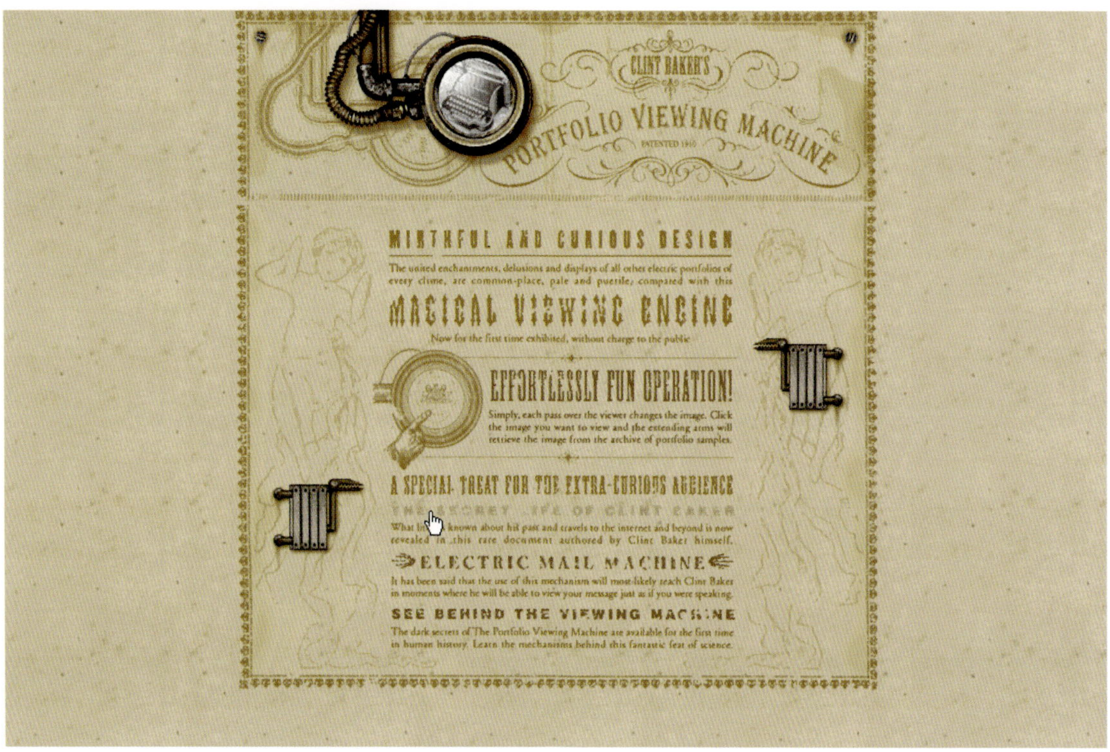

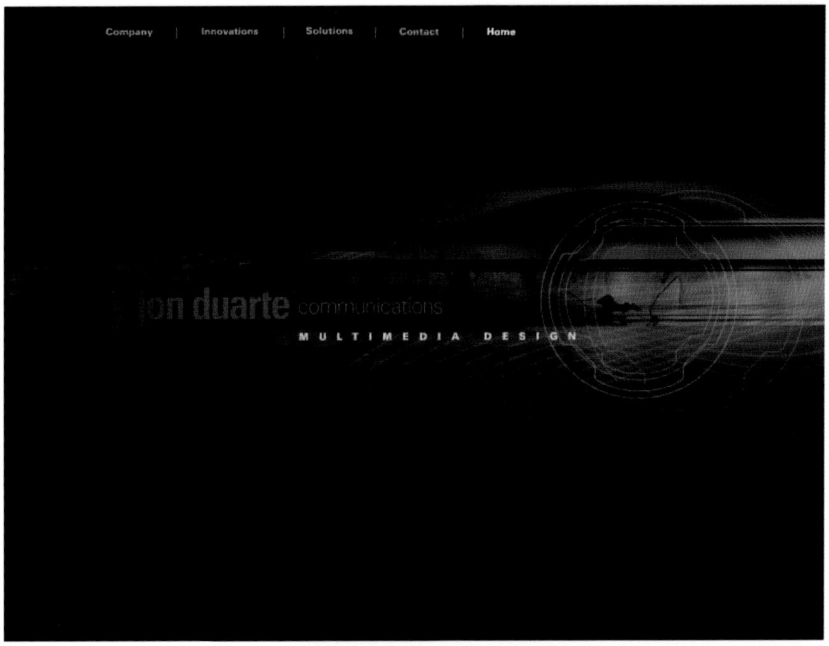

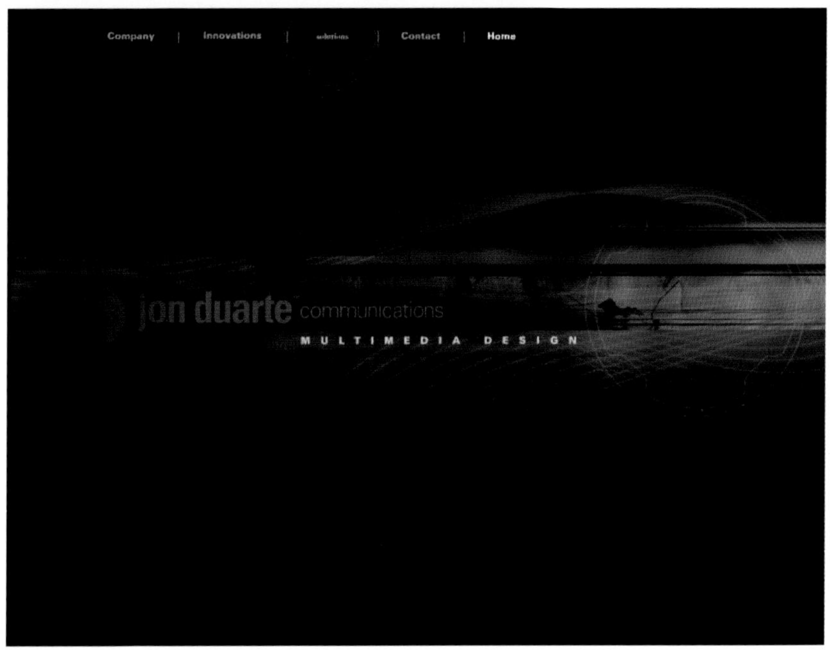

Title
Jon Duarte
URL
www.jonduarte.com/
Design Firm
Jon Duarte Communications

This high-tech homepage contains all the information that you need in a small, well-designed space. Shapes move subtly in the background, giving life to the whole design.

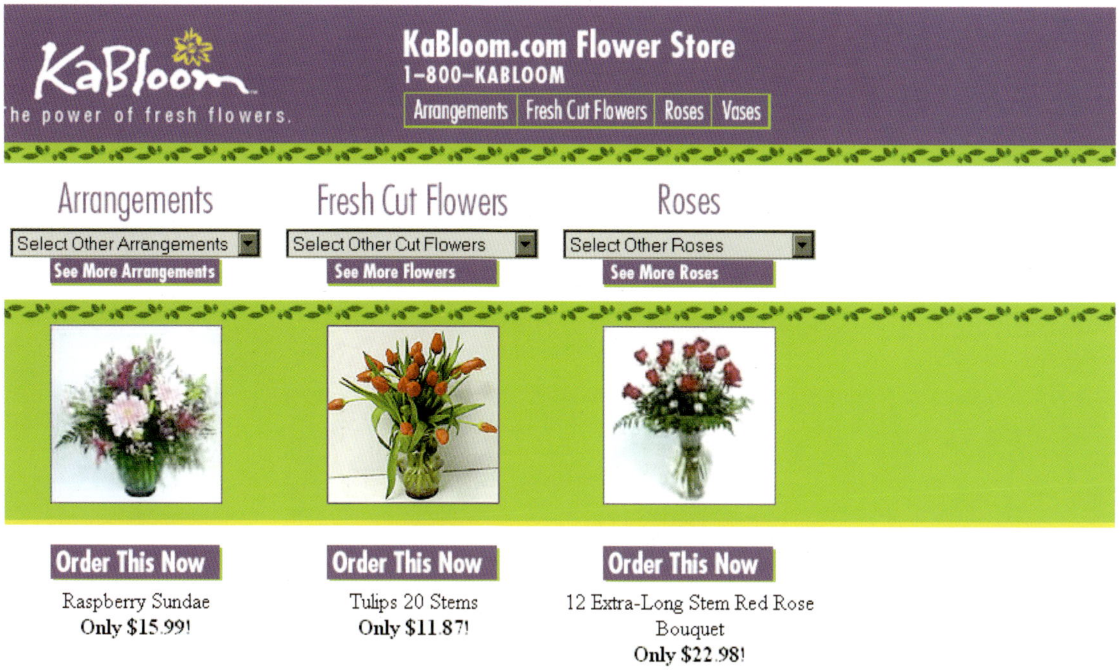

Title
KaBloom
URL
www.kabloom.com/
Design firm
KaBloom

E-commerce does not have to look bad, although most e-commerce sites do. KaBloom avoids the most common pitfalls, such as boring colors and lack of an integrated design.

Title
petergrafik
URL
www.petergrafik.dk/
Design firm
petergrafik/space time foam
Designer
peter Holm

When was the last time you saw a Web site that featured a brown motif? Petergrafik has a look all its own, with simple iconic illustrations serving as buttons and an overall design sense that is too rare on the Internet.

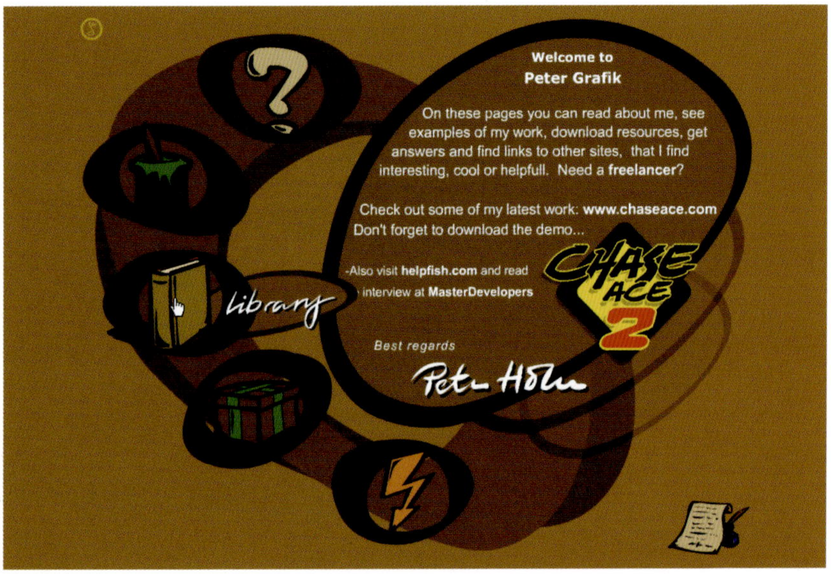

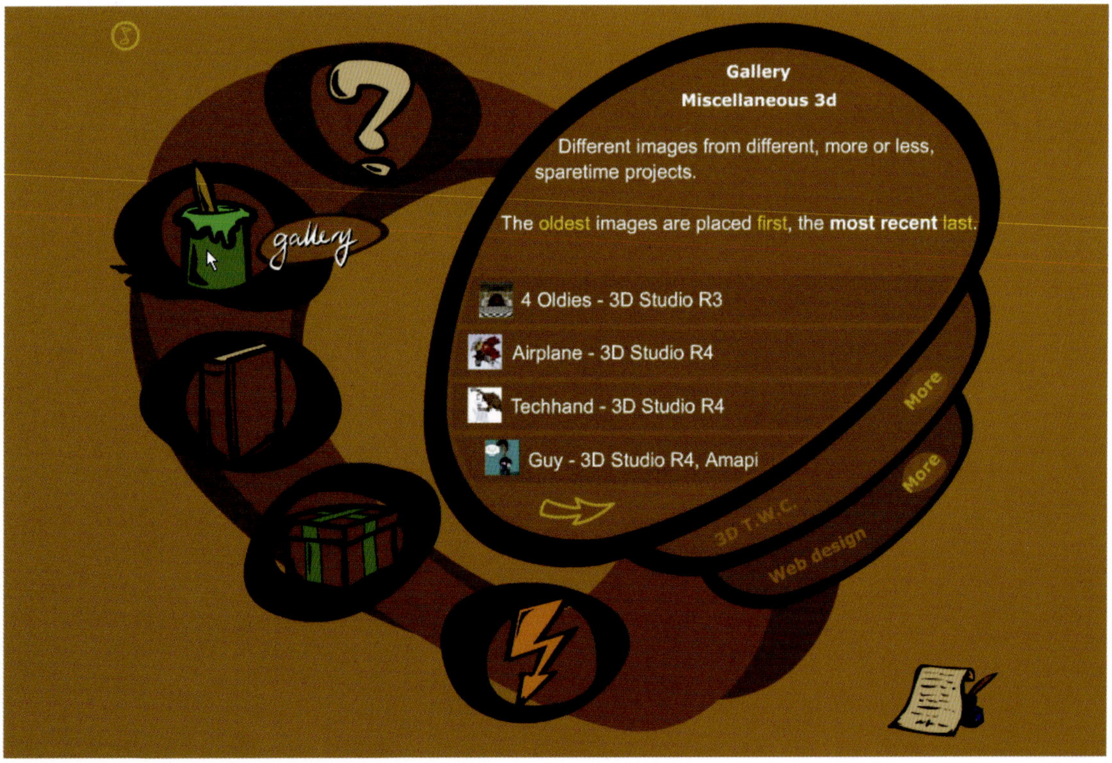

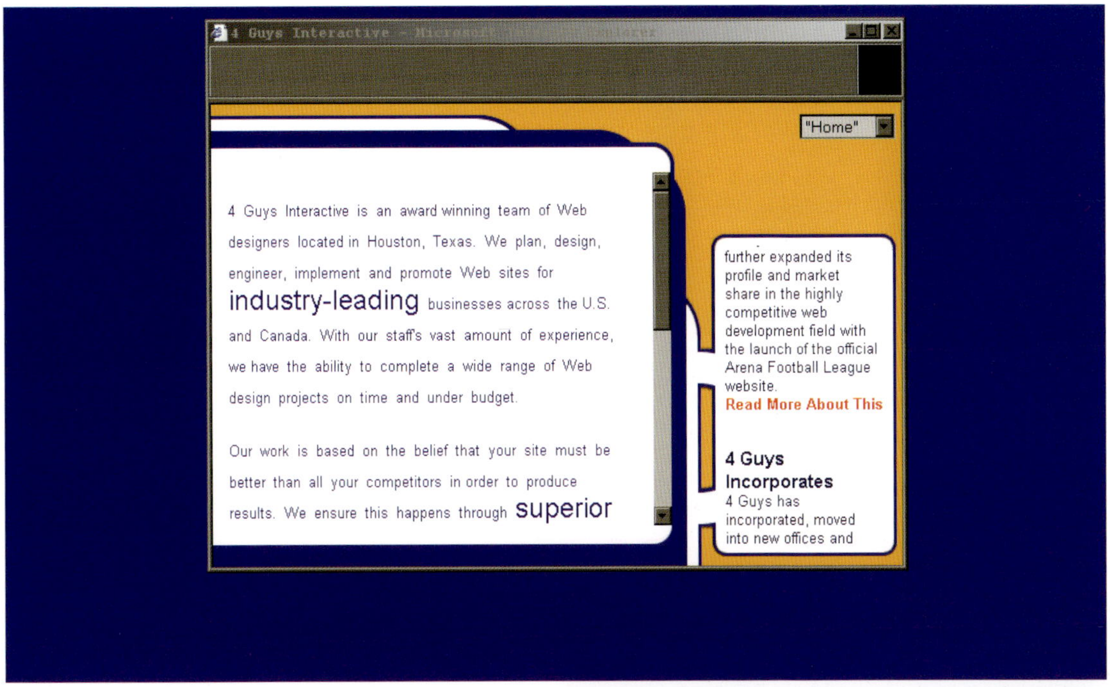

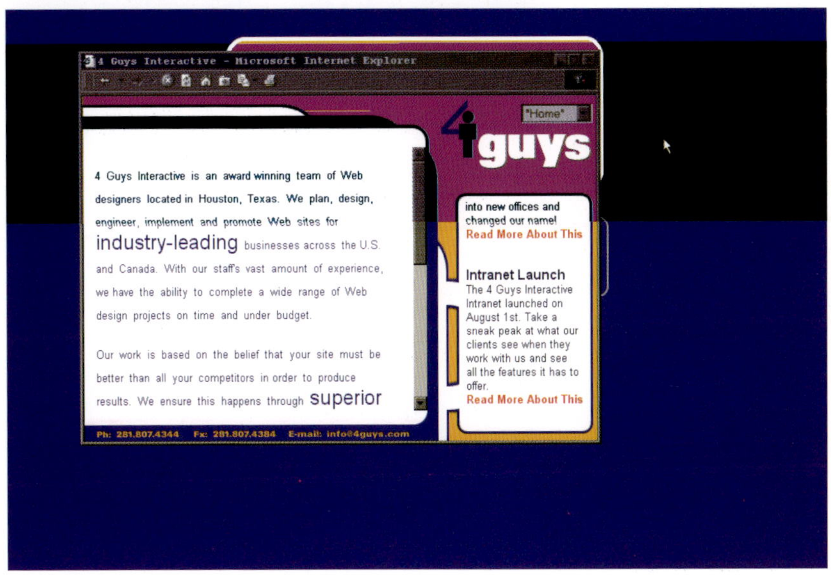

Title
4 guys
URL
www.4guys.com/
Design Firm
4 guys interactive

The 4 Guys homepage features a blend of Macromedia Flash with frames. Containing as many as eight frames within the pop-up window, this site clarifies what could have been a confusing amount of information.

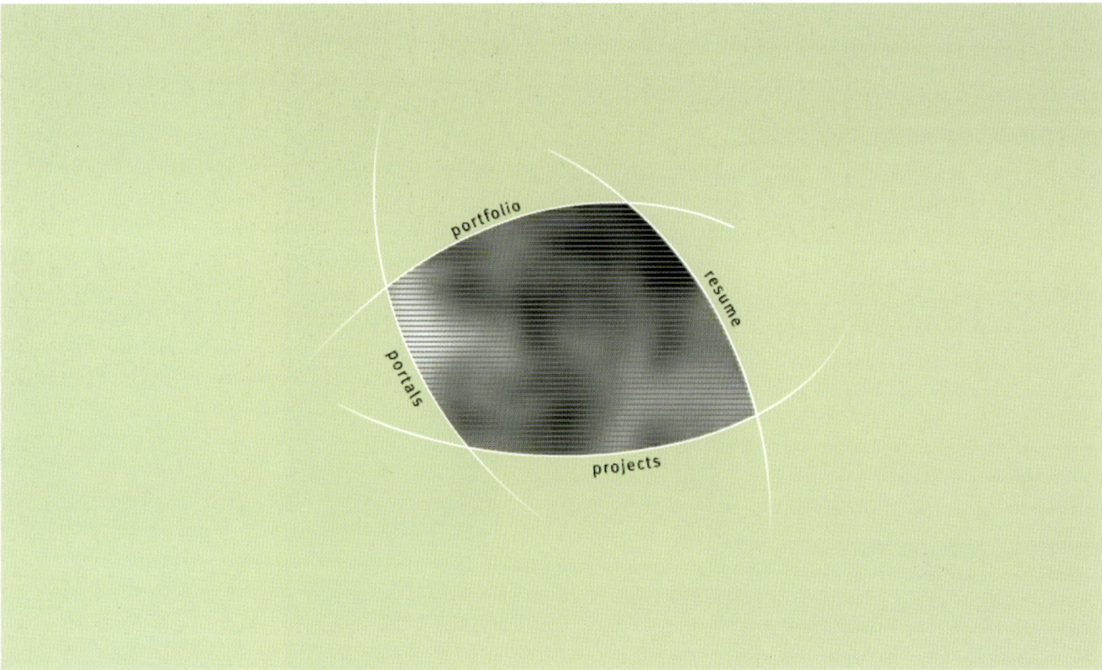

Title
Andy Lim
URL
andy.artdirectors.com/
Design Firm
Embedded Wireless Labs

Andy Lim's homepage combines muted colors and animated buttons to create a good-looking site. Lim doesn't go overboard with this Flash-generated site, but the movement is just enough to maintain interest.

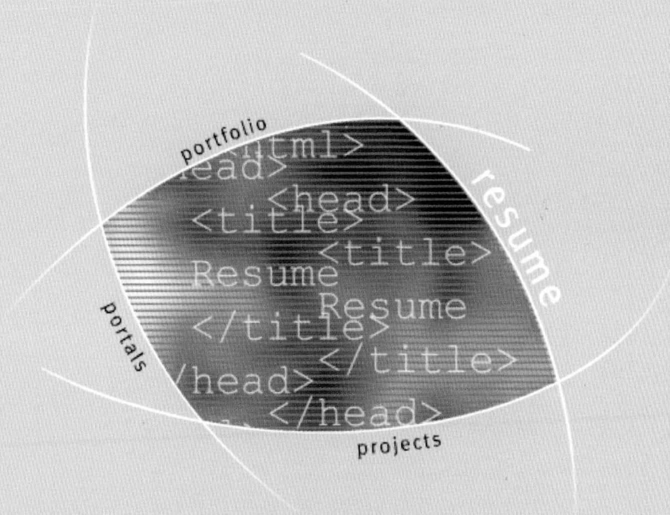
portfolio
resume
portals
projects
<html>
<head>
<title>
<title>
Resume
Resume
</title>
</title>
/head>
</head>

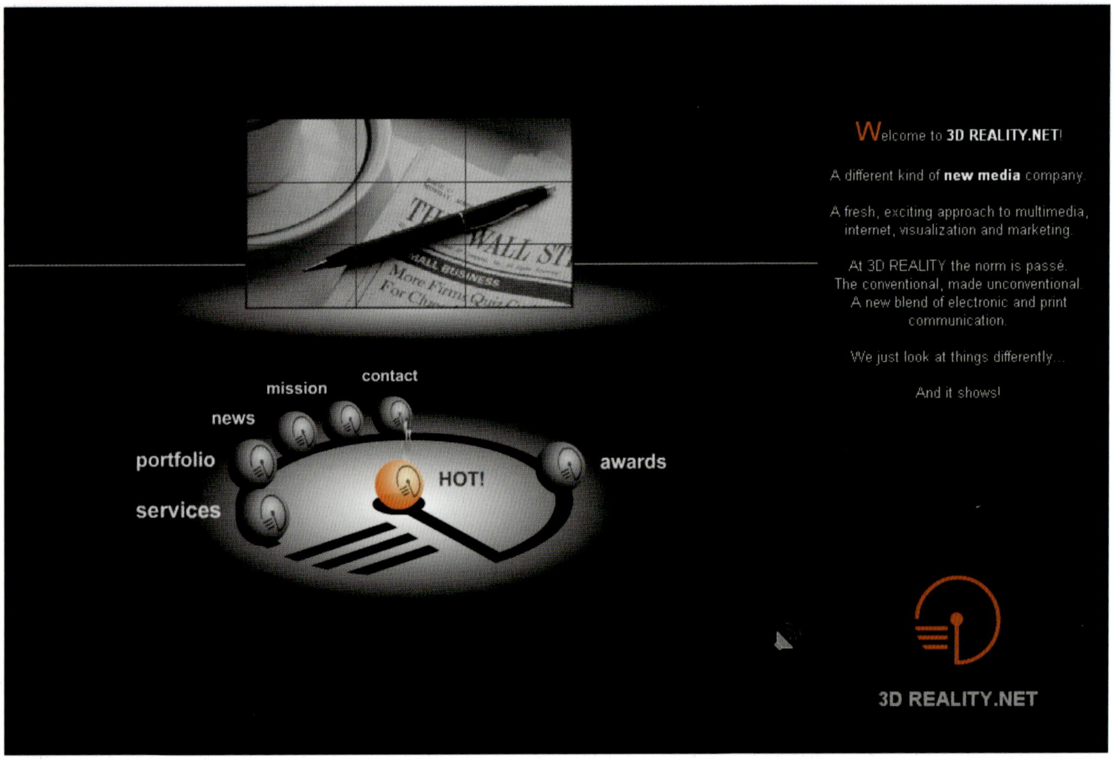

Title
3D Reality
URL
www.3dreality.net/main.html
Design Firm
3D Reality.net
Designers
Les Fram, R. Tyler Smith

The Flash-enabled homepage of 3D Reality features a spotlight on the buttons and a "hot" button that goes to "hotter" on mouse-over. The feeling of a large, important boardroom gives the site a professional gloss.

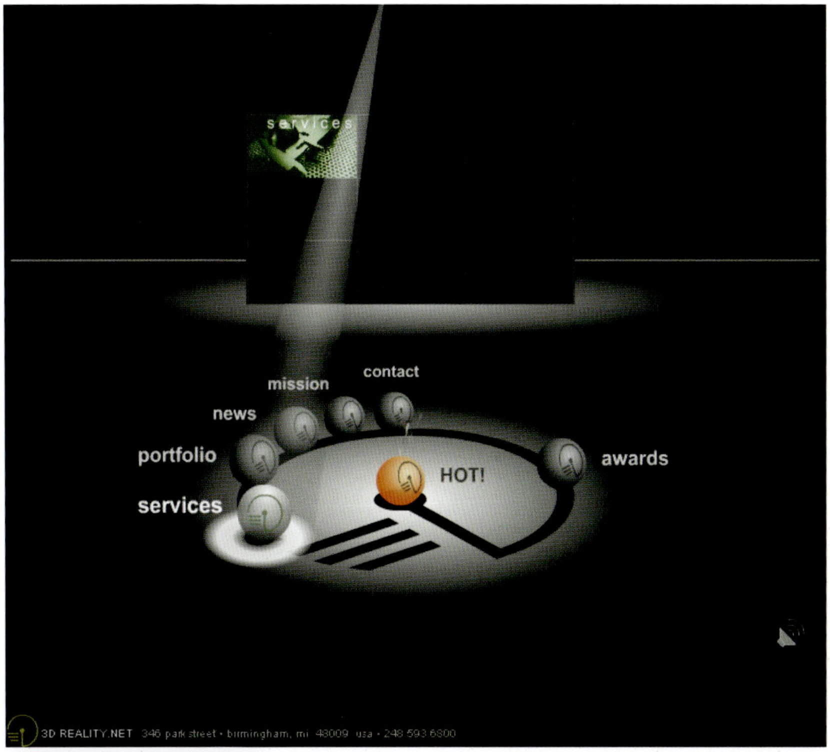
services
mission
contact
news
portfolio
HOT!
awards
services
3D REALITY.NET 346 park street • birmingham, mi 48009 usa • 248.593.6800

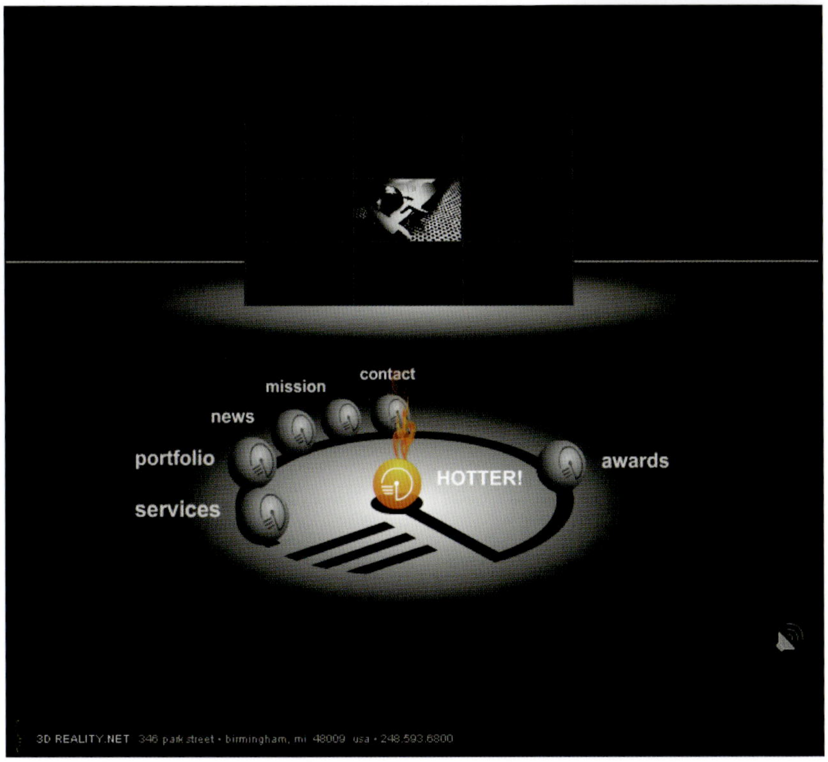
mission
contact
news
portfolio
HOTTER!
awards
services
3D REALITY.NET 346 park street • birmingham, mi 48009 usa • 248.593.6800

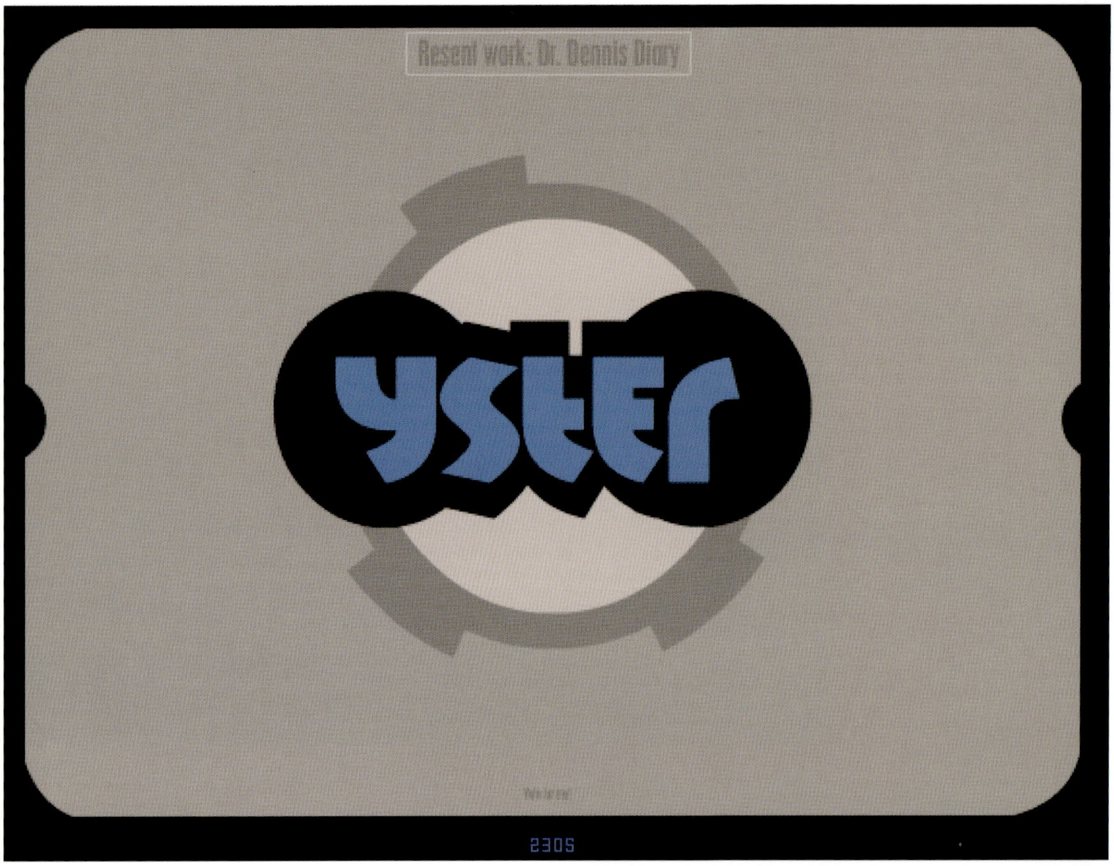

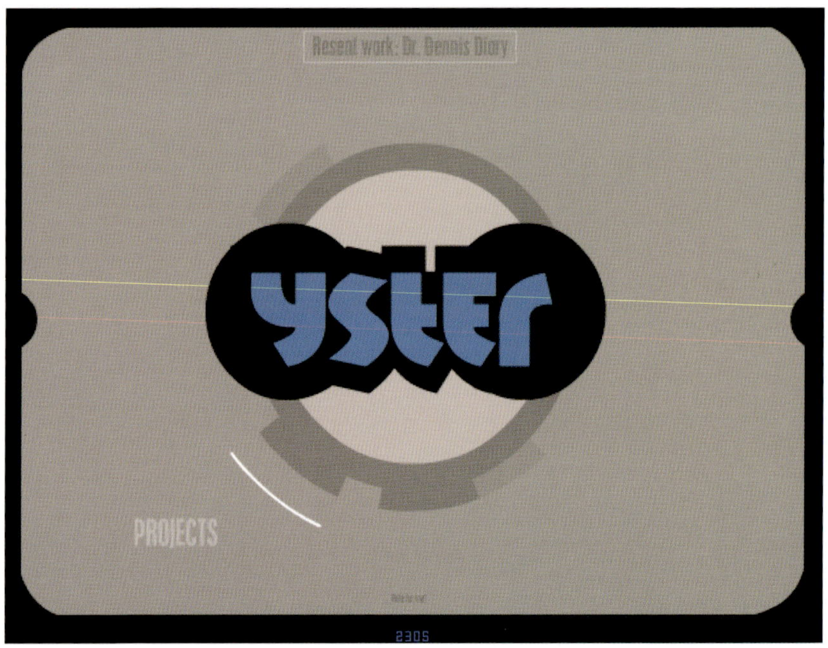

Title
yster
URL
yster.just.nu
Design firm
SLB Interactive

The centerpiece of this subdued design is three animated buttons. Nothing about this site hits you over the head; even the text fits smoothly into the background.

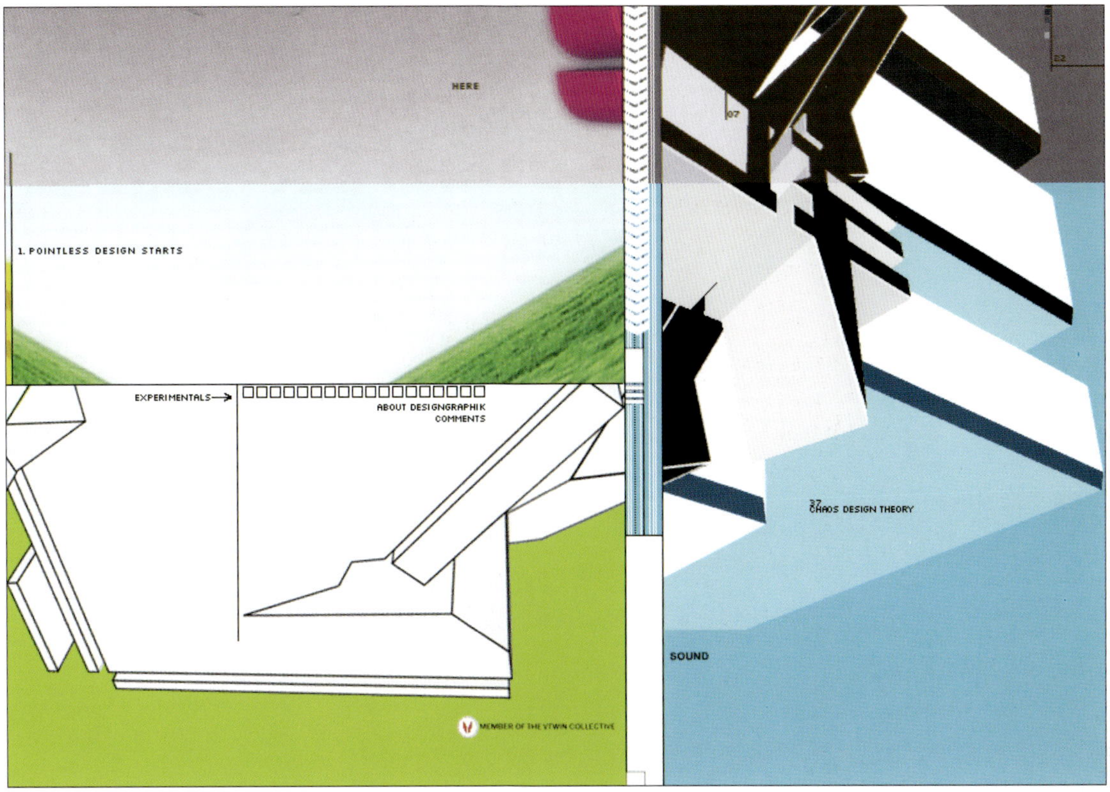

Title
Designgraphik
URL
www.designgraphik.com/
Design firm
Designgraphik
Designer
Mike Young

The splashpage for the Designgraphik site is ambiguous and somewhat confusing, but for this experimental site, that works well.

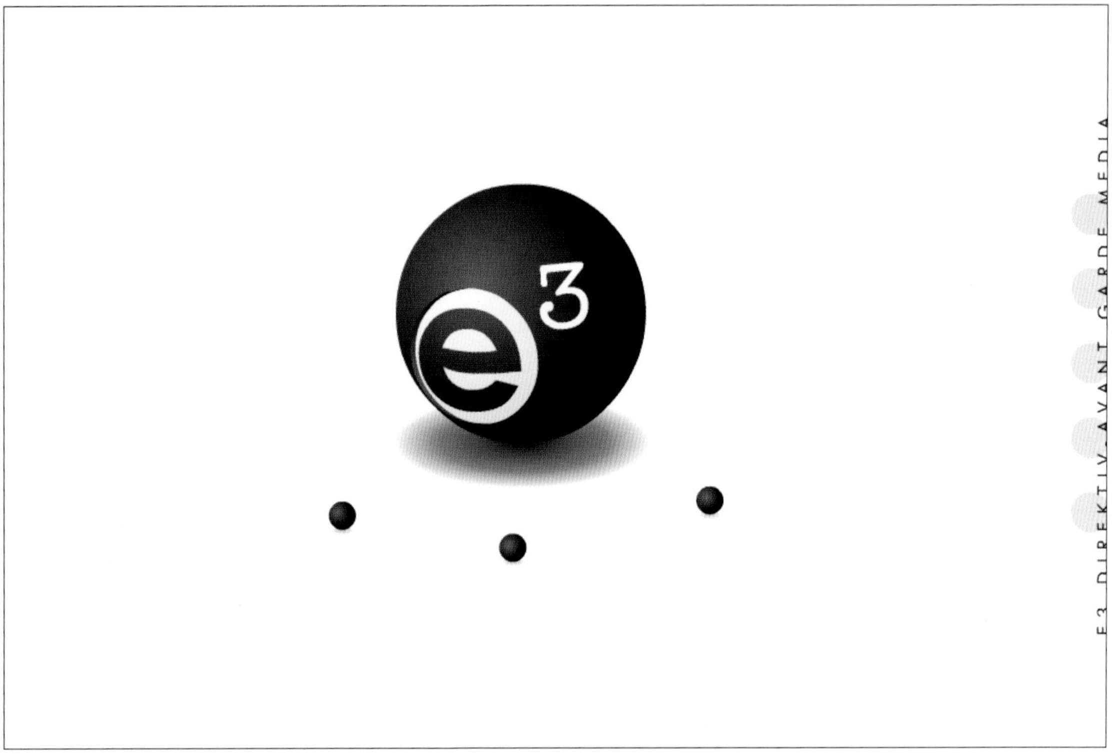

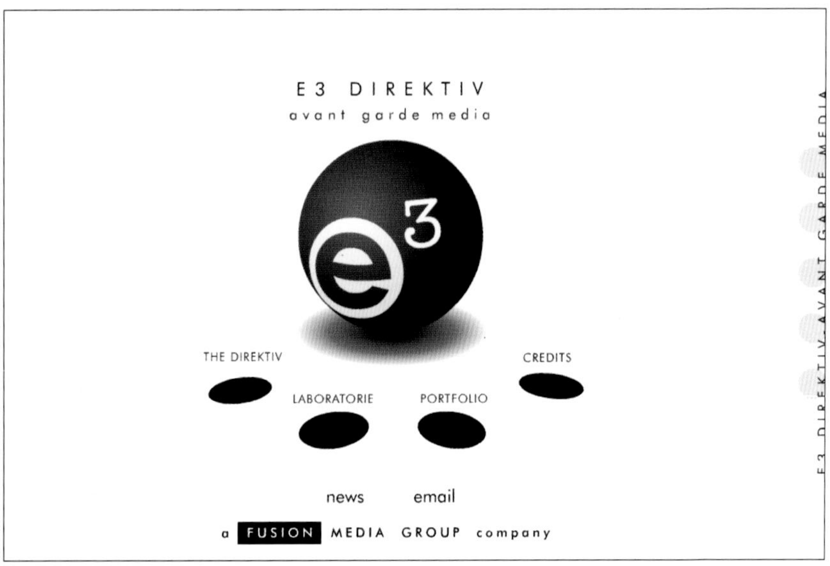

Title
E3 Direktiv
URL
www.envisioninteractive.com
Design Firm
Envision Interactive
Designer
Fusion Media Group, Inc., Elmer Erana, producer

This homepage features the great E3 logo. The ball appears to roll out and spit out smaller balls that become the links. The eight-ball logo remains the focus of attention.

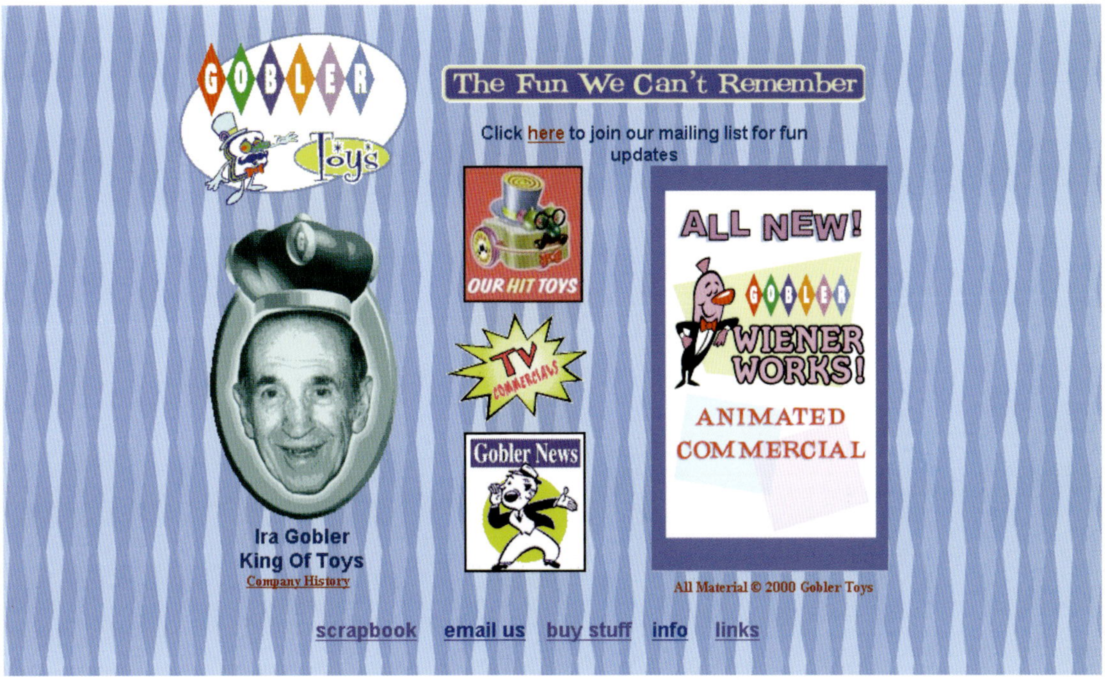

title
gobler toys
URL
www.goblertoys.com/
design firm
gobler toys
designer
steven casino

A retro look is achieved by the use of kitschy, fifties colors and patterns. This a site that underscores an Internet trend, looking to the past, when print media had restrictions in aspects like color, just the way the Web does today.

Title
Me company
URL
www.mecompany.com/
Design firm
Me company
[Designer/tk]

Buttons that highlight on mouse-over with a big block of color on the side combine to make a homepage that works from both a usability sense and from a design sense.

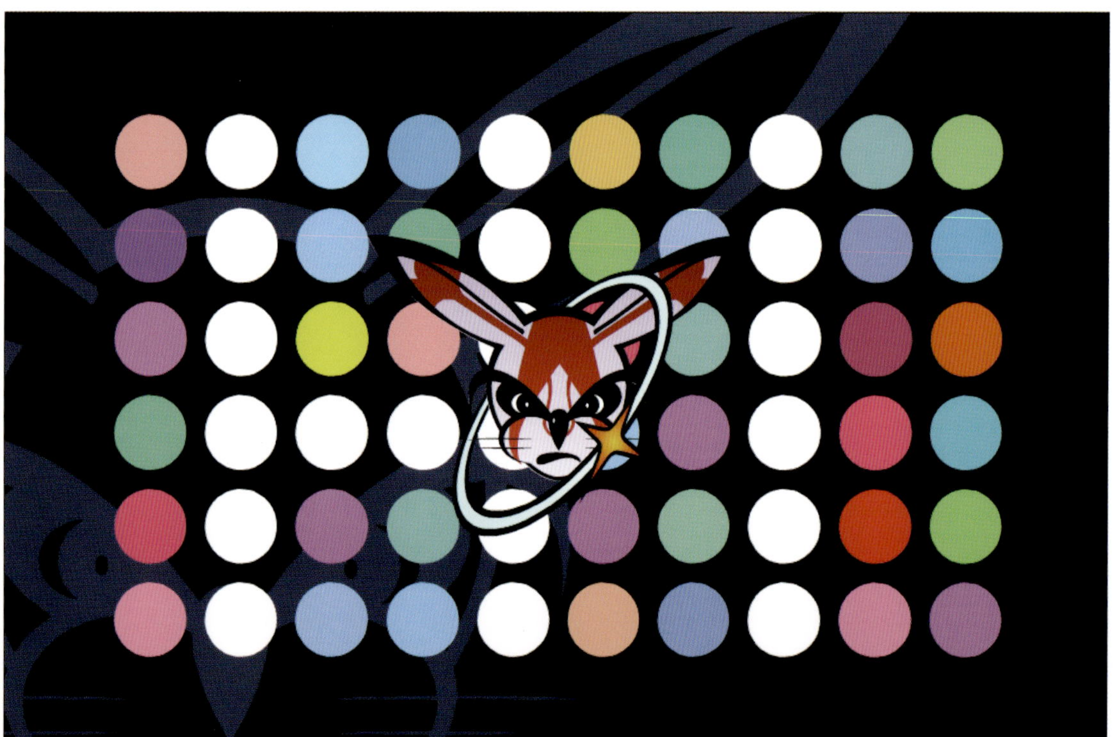

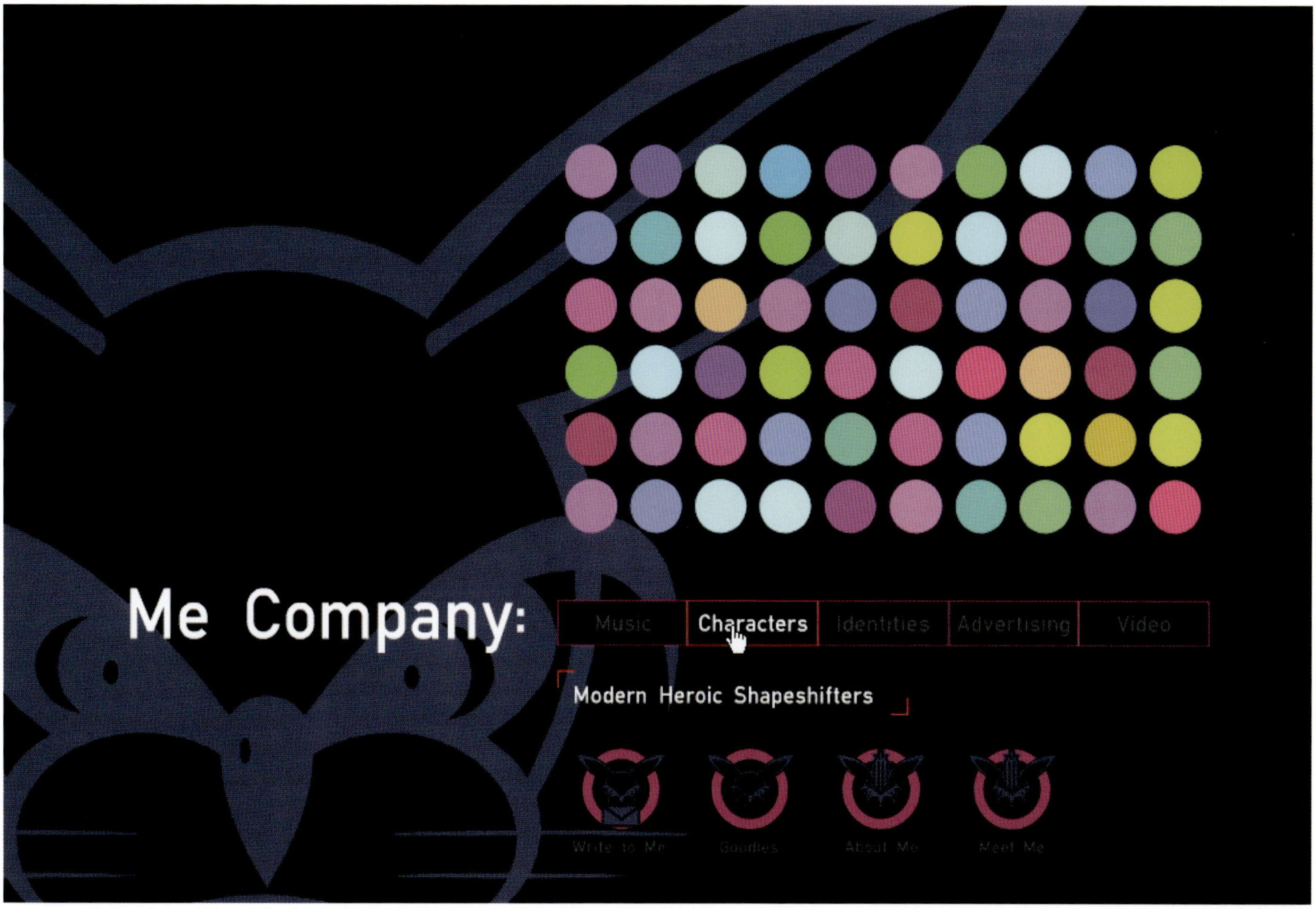
Me Company:
Music
Characters
Identities
Advertising
Video
Modern Heroic Shapeshifters
Write to Me
Goodies
About Me
Meet Me

Title
ABI Mouldings
URL
www.abimouldings.com/
Design Firm
ABI Mouldings

This slick homepage has all the necessary navigation buttons off to one side, with the company's philosophy taking center stage over a cool, modern background.

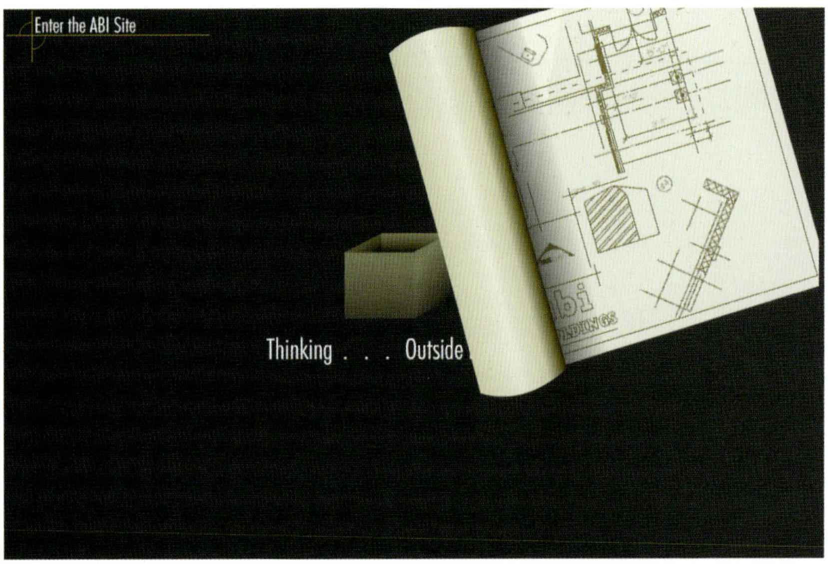

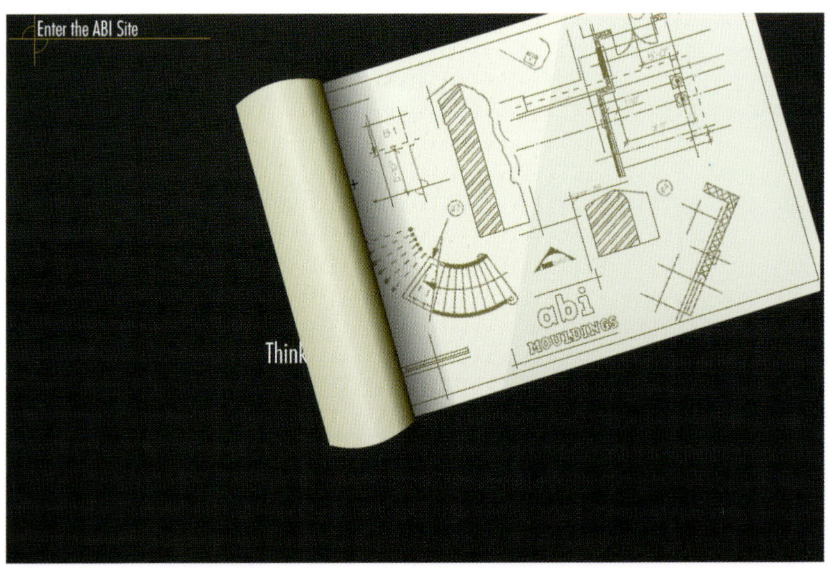

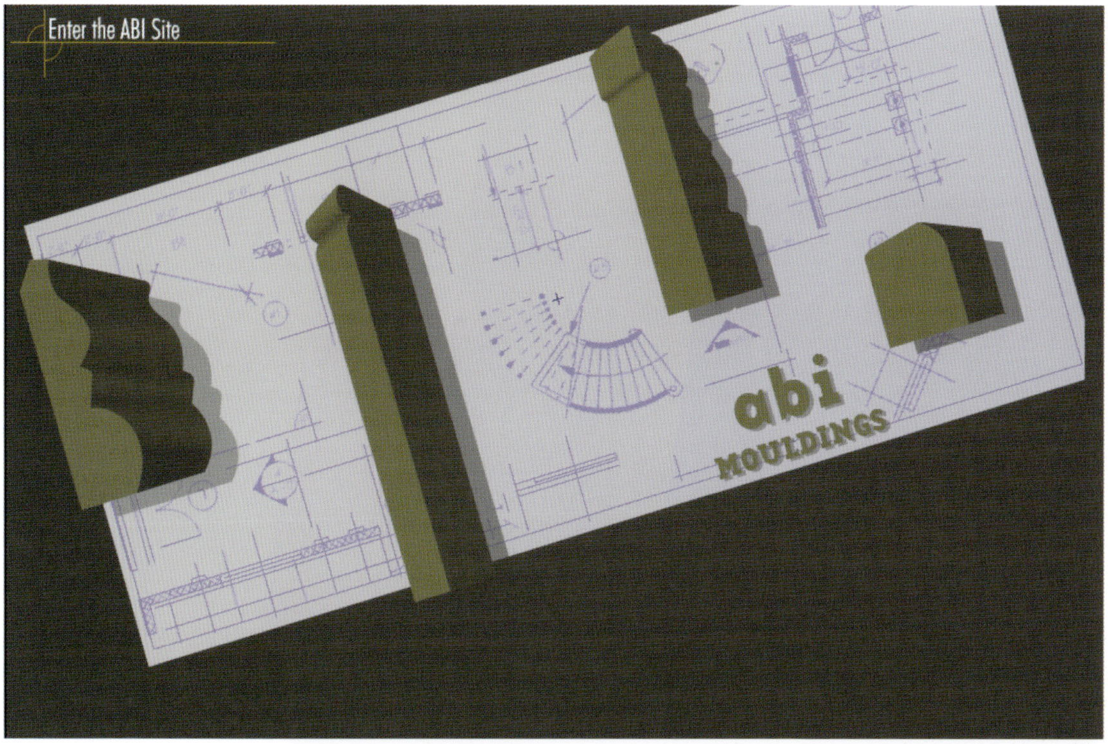
Enter the ABI Site
abi
MOULDINGS

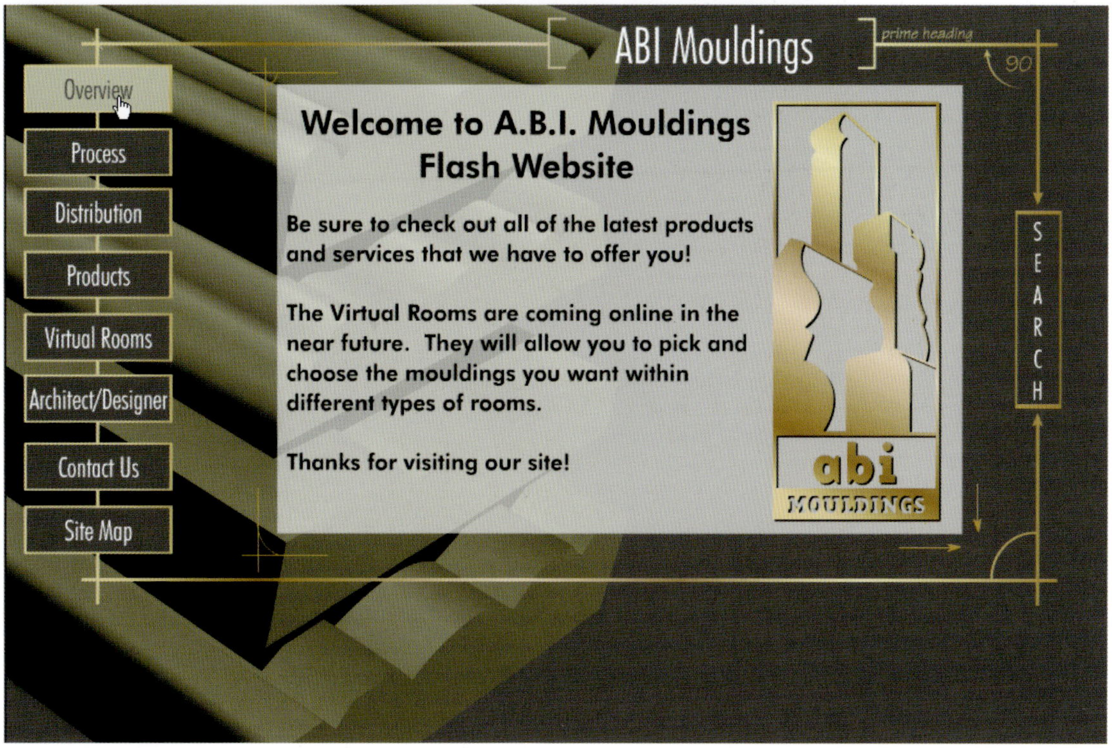
ABI Mouldings
prime heading
90
Overview
Process
Distribution
Products
Virtual Rooms
Architect/Designer
Contact Us
Site Map
Welcome to A.B.I. Mouldings Flash Website
Be sure to check out all of the latest products and services that we have to offer you!
The Virtual Rooms are coming online in the near future. They will allow you to pick and choose the mouldings you want within different types of rooms.
Thanks for visiting our site!
abi
MOULDINGS
SEARCH

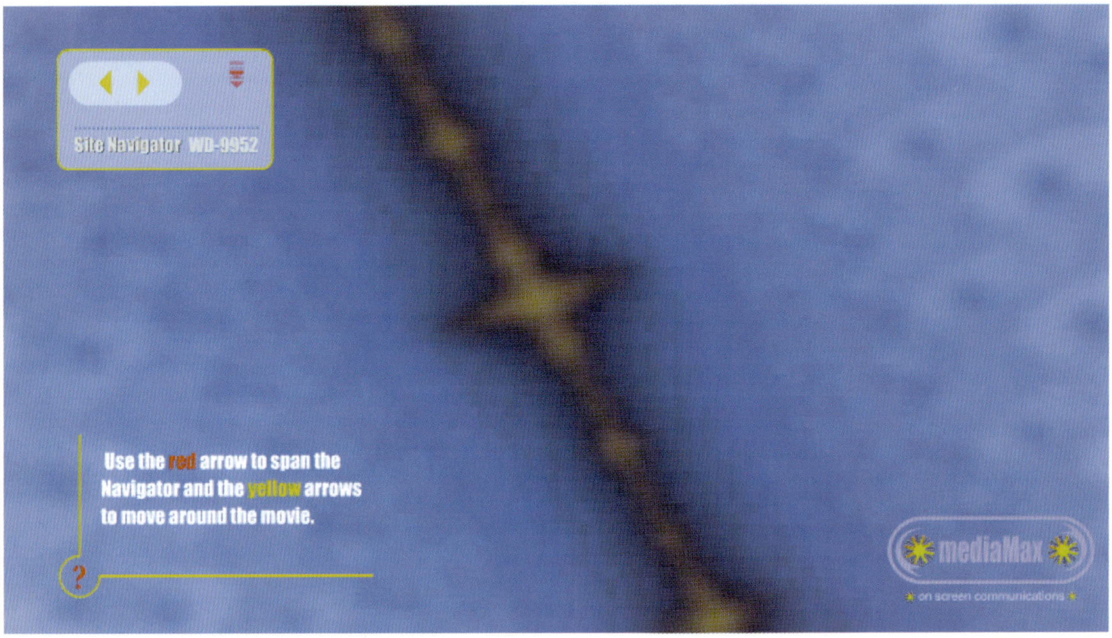

Title
Mediamax
URL
www.mediamax.gr
Design firm
Mediamax

This homepage features a drop-down console interface that makes navigation easy and maximizes the design area. The fuzzy, close-up photos and illustrations remain the focus.

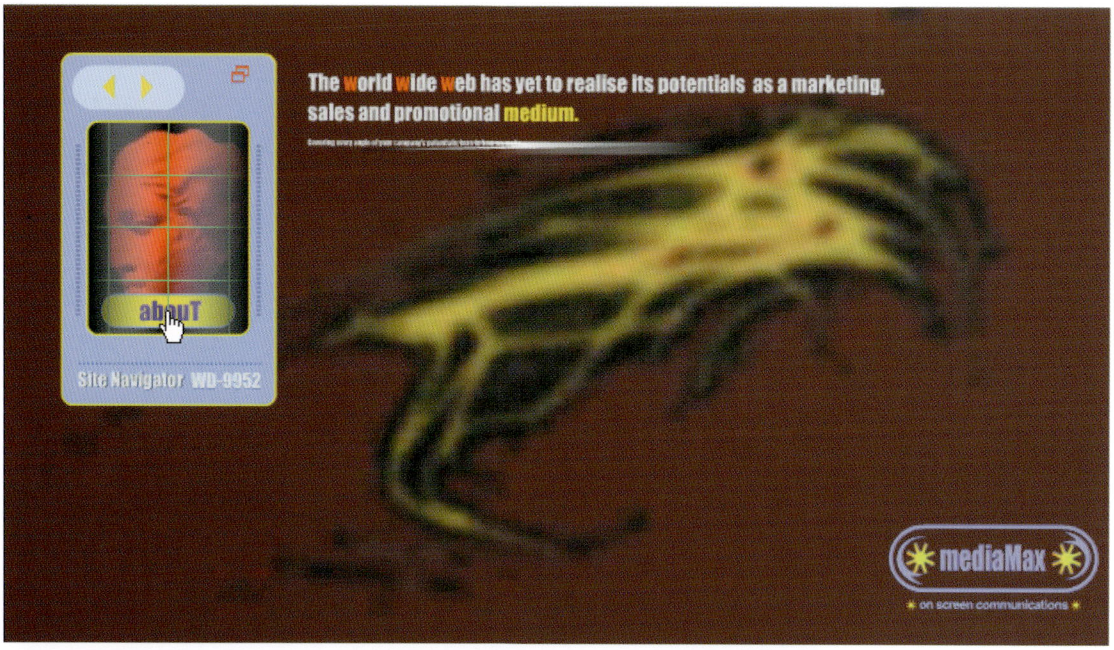
The world wide web has yet to realise its potentials as a marketing, sales and promotional medium.
abouT
Site Navigator WD-9952
mediaMax
on screen communications

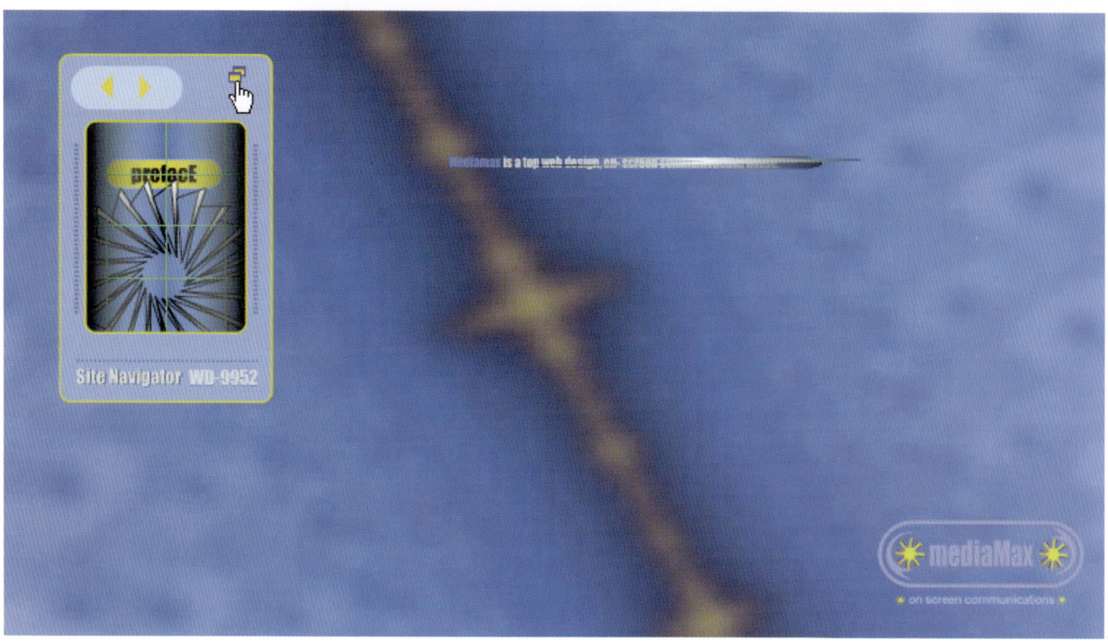
Site Navigator WD-9952
mediaMax
on screen communications

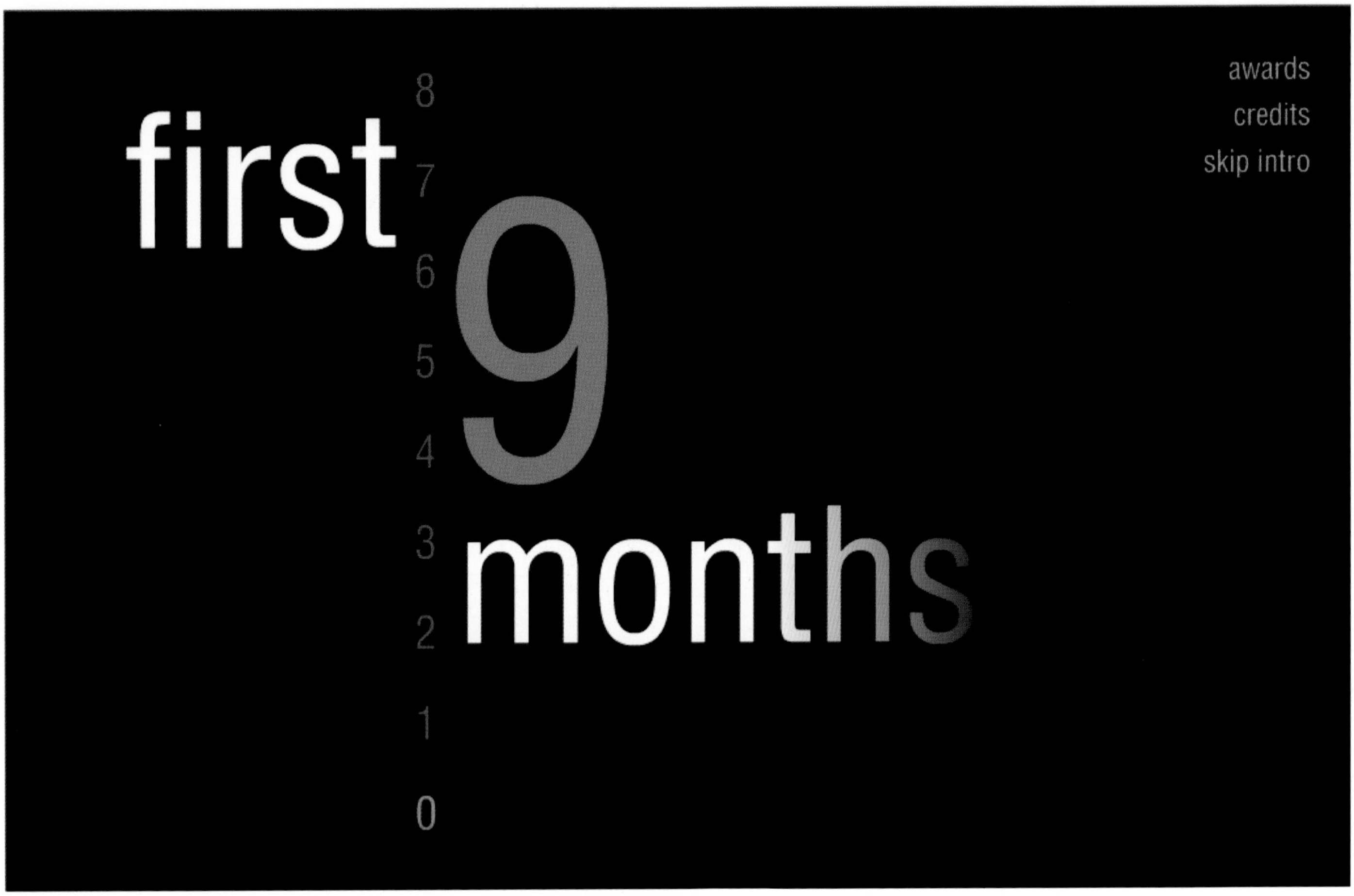

Title
first 9 Months
URL
www.first9months.com/
Design Firm
12 south.com
Designer
Joseph Moore

An interactive journey through the first nine months of a baby's life begins with a page that features a countdown to the baby. The 0 is an animated button and leads to the rest of this well-designed site.

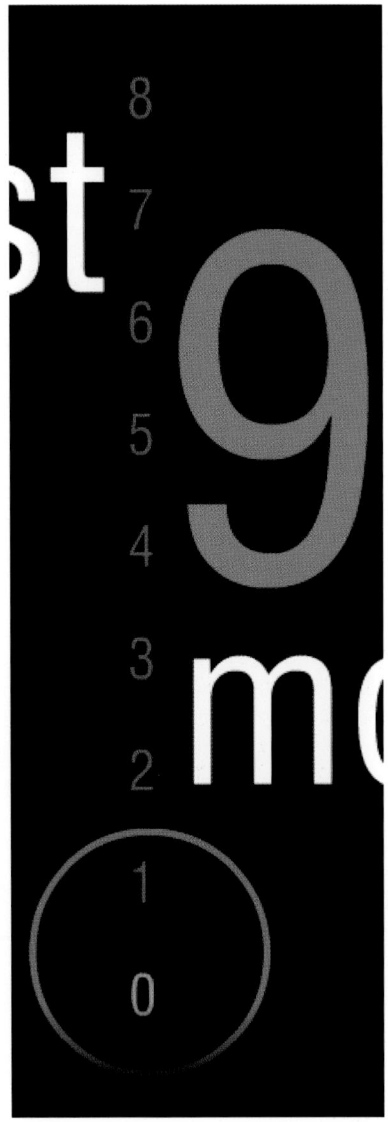

st
8
7
6
5
4
3
2
1
0

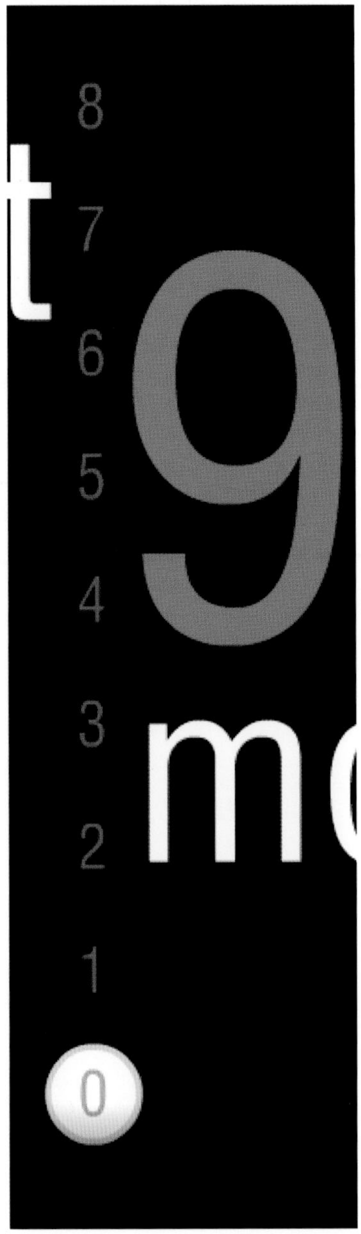

t
8
7
6
5
4
3
2
1
0

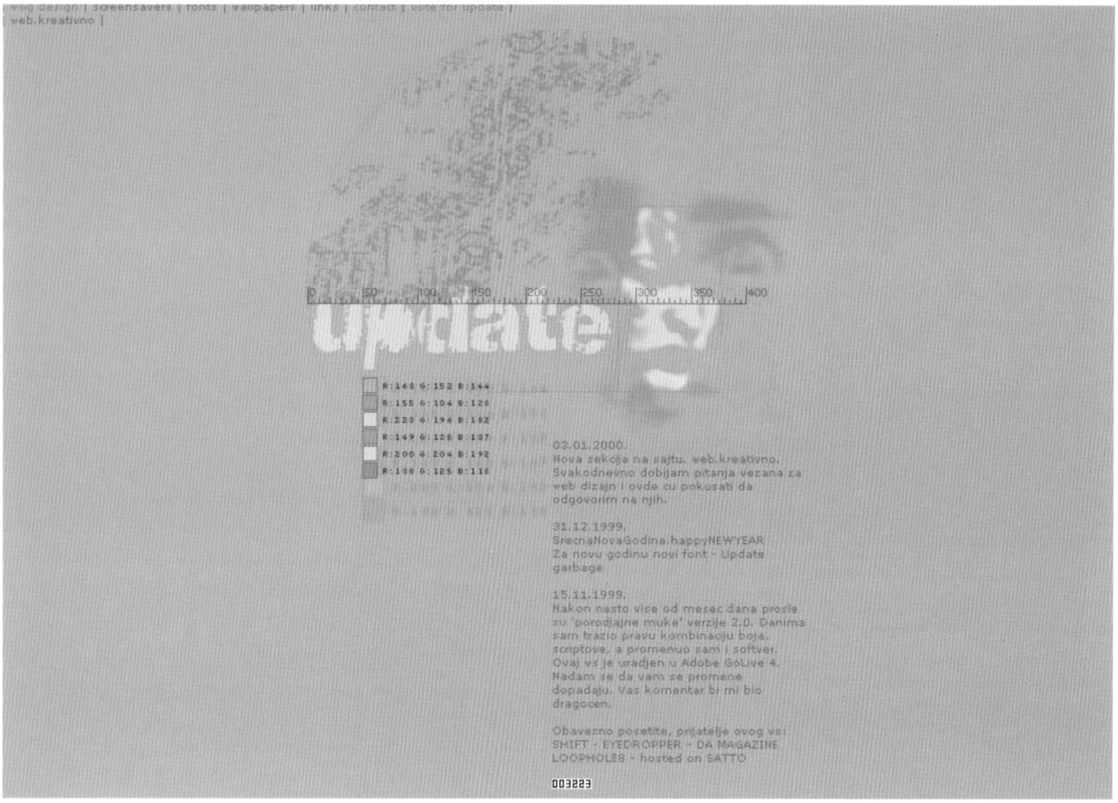

Title
Goran Design
URL
www.gorandesign.com/index.html
Design Firm
Goran Design

The muted colors on the Goran site are very viewer-friendly. The splashpage gets your attention without knocking you over the head. The illustrations are also interesting.

Title
Netgraphic
URL
www.netgraphic.ch/
Design Firm
Audiobox Klangkonzepte

The Netgraphic homepage features a shadowed navigation bar that appears to be suspended in midair. This is a look that has yet to gain popularity on the Internet, but you will see more and more of this, for obvious reasons.

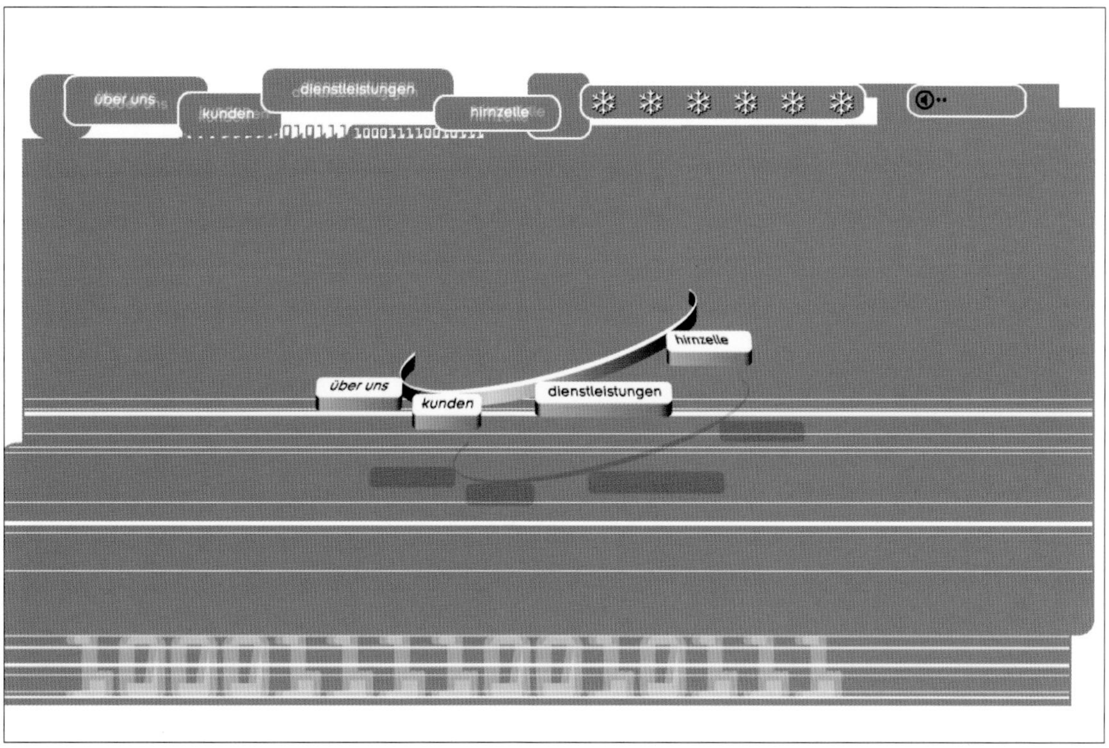

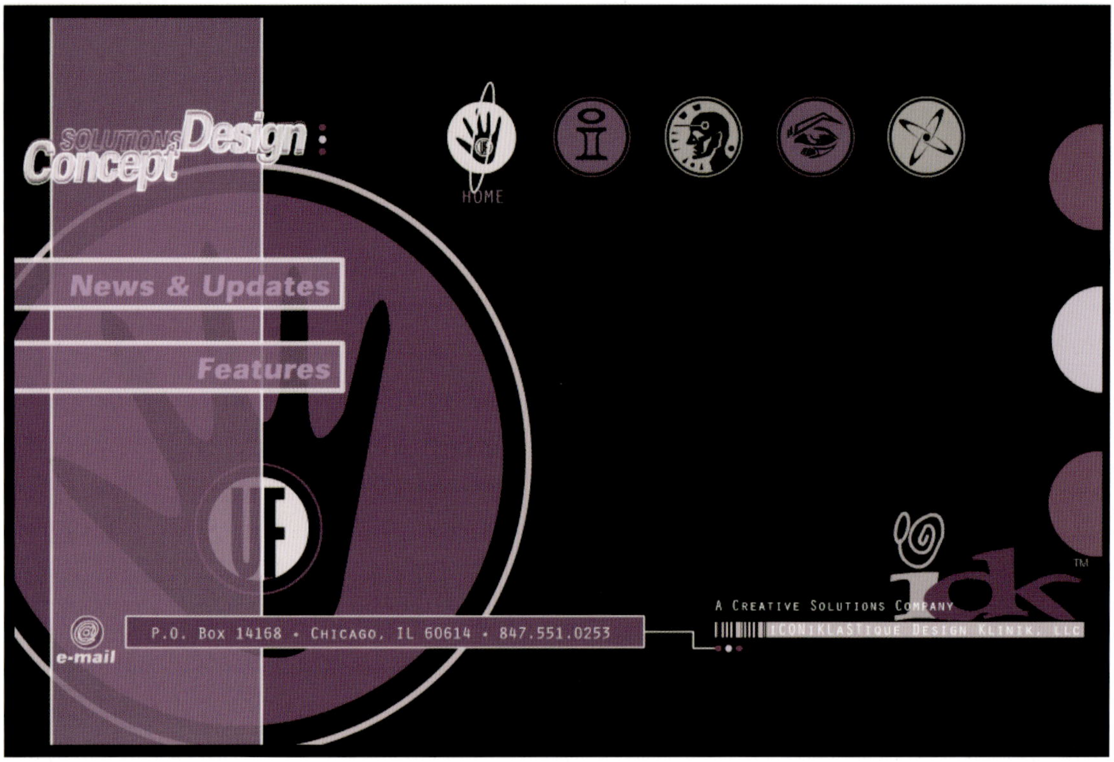

Title
Iconiklastique
URL
www.ida-a-ok.com/
Design Firm
Iconiklastique Design Klinik, LLC

Many buttons and submenus don't overwhelm this homepage because of the mouse-over navigation and the intelligent design. Iconiklastique has created a template for good sites.

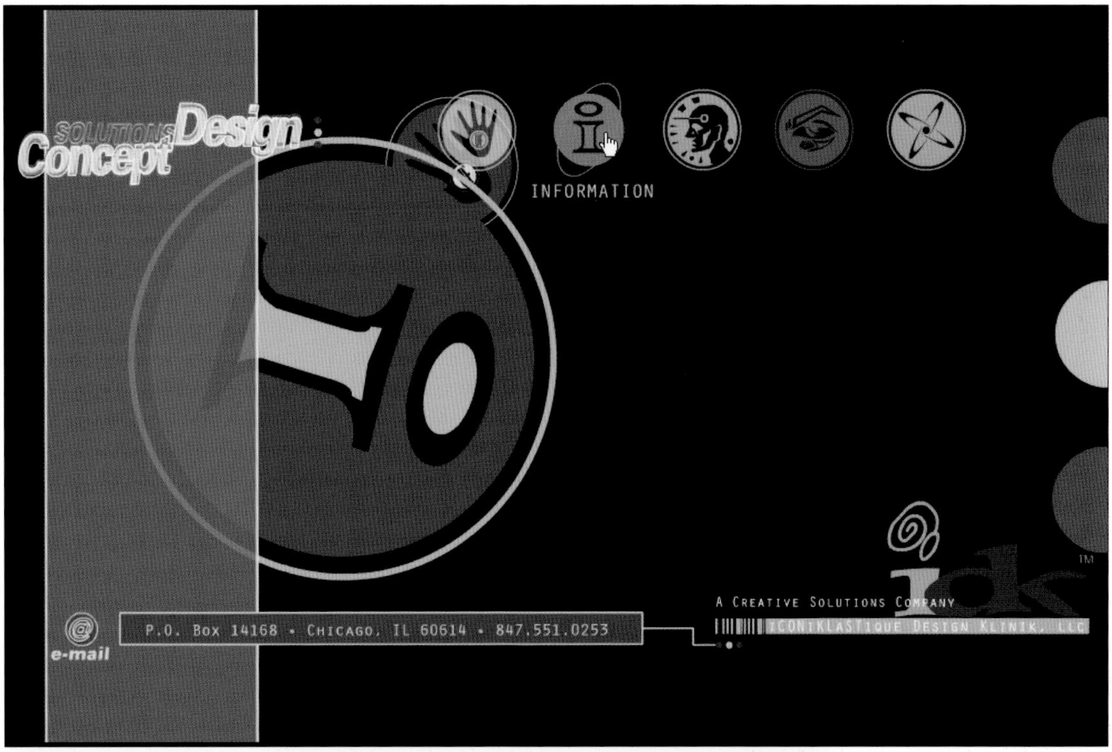

SOLUTIONS Design Concept
INFORMATION
A CREATIVE SOLUTIONS COMPANY
ICONIKLASTIQUE DESIGN KLINIK, LLC
P.O. Box 14168 • Chicago, IL 60614 • 847.551.0253
e-mail

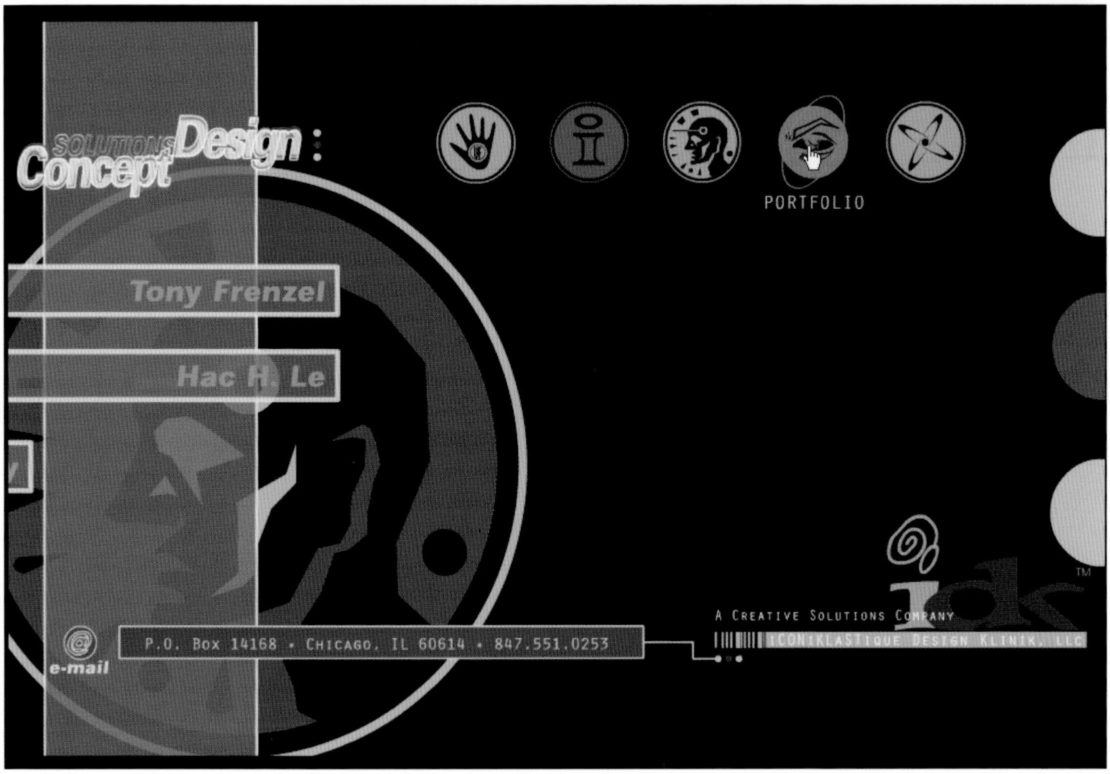

SOLUTIONS Design Concept
PORTFOLIO
Tony Frenzel
Hac H. Le
A CREATIVE SOLUTIONS COMPANY
ICONIKLASTIQUE DESIGN KLINIK, LLC
P.O. Box 14168 • Chicago, IL 60614 • 847.551.0253
e-mail

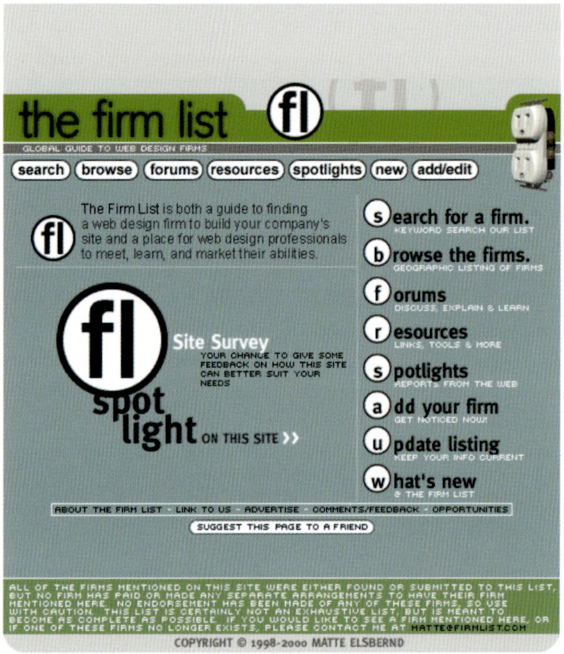

Title
The Firm List
URL
thefirmlist.com/main.html
Design Firm
The Firm List

If you are going to try to make a comprehensive list of Web-design companies, then you had better design your Web site well. At The Firm List, they have done just that. Lots of buttons don't overwhelm, and the color scheme looks professional and inviting.

Title
superesc
URL
www.superesc.com/
Design Firm
superesc
Designer
calvin sun

Animated .gifs add some movement to Calvin Sun's homepage. The look of the site is original, something like photocopier art.

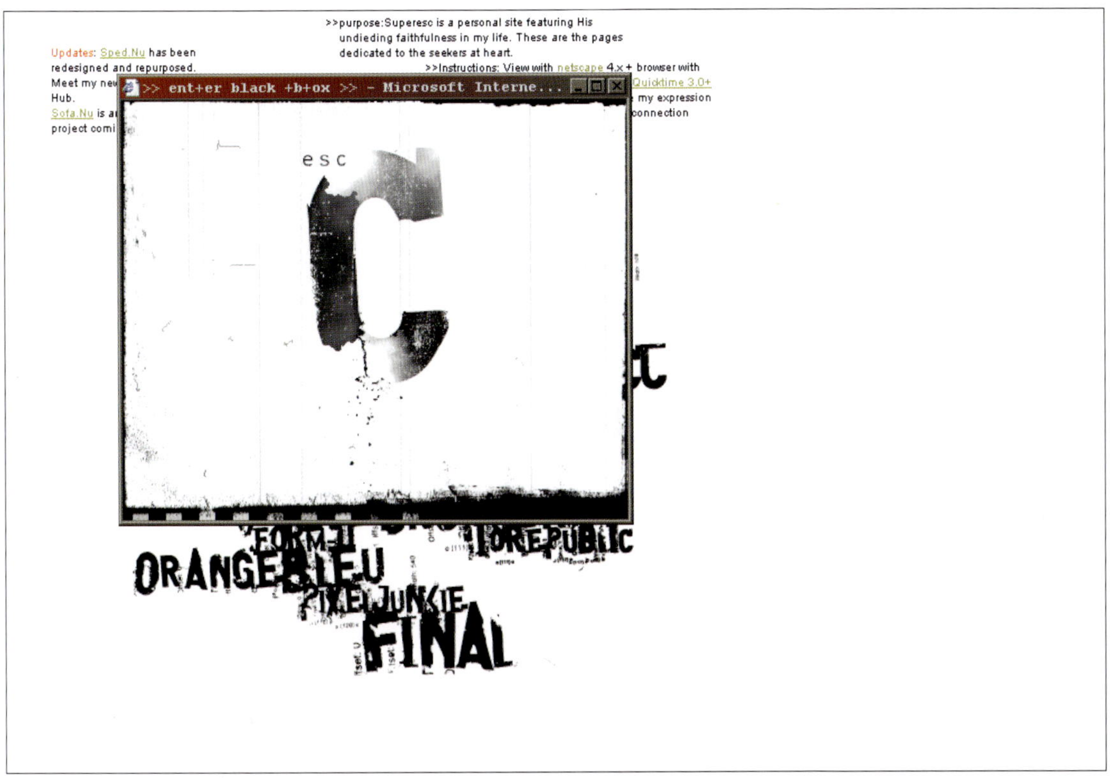

Title
KVAD.com
URL
vatne@online.no
Design firm
KVAD.com

Bright orange grabs your attention immediately on this homepage. The centerpiece illustration is cool, and the philosophy of the site is right below the buttons. Animated .gifs add movement.

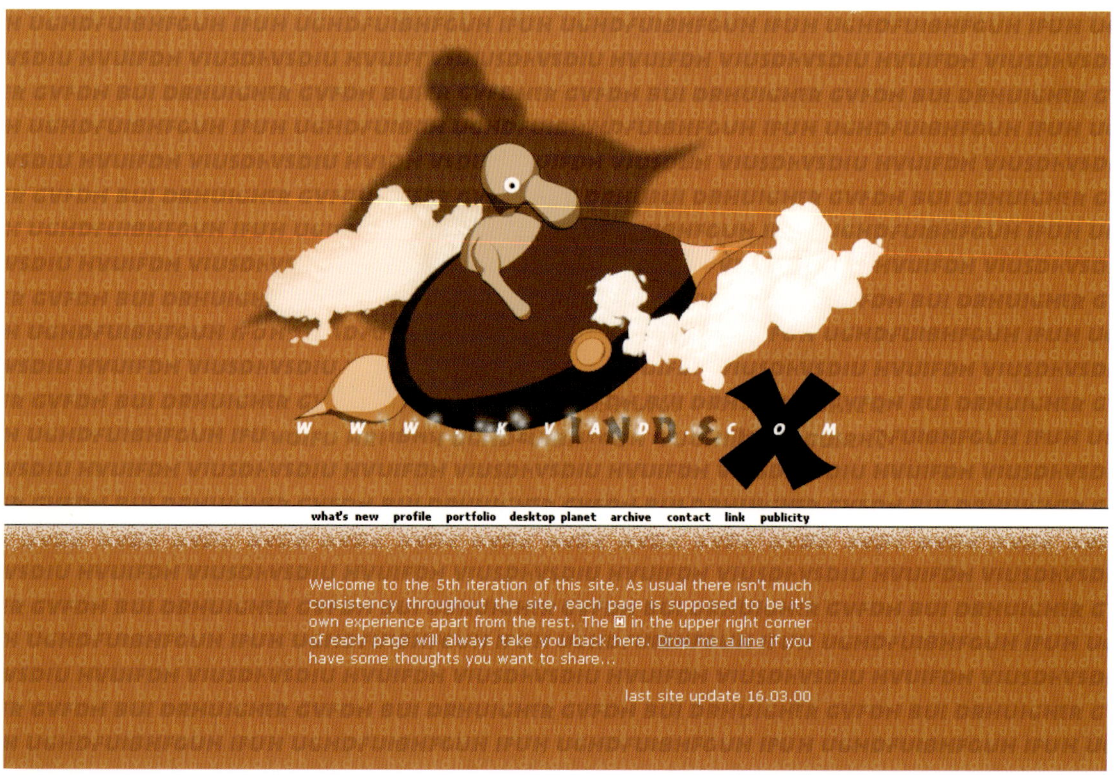

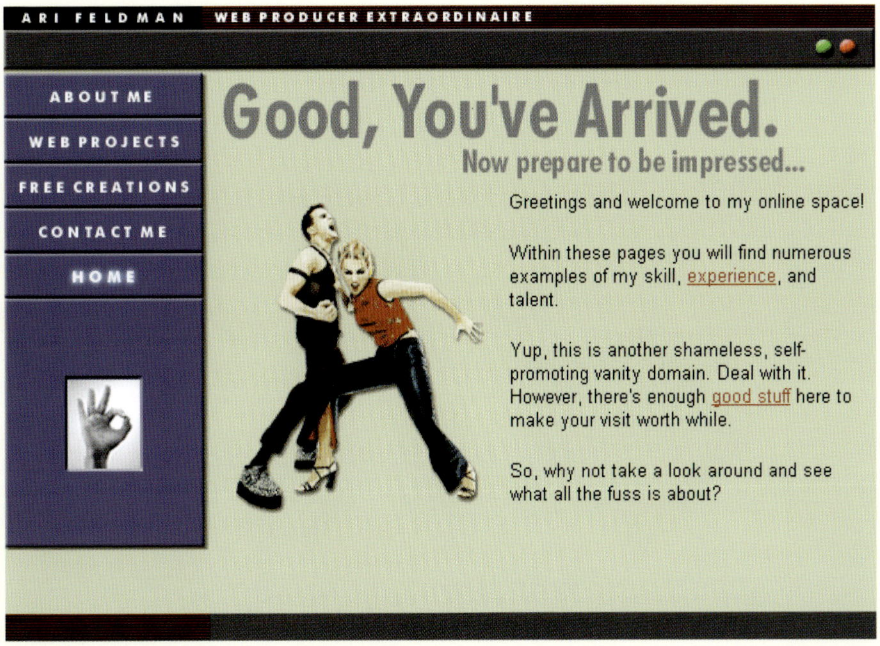

Title
Ari Feldman
URL
www.arifeldman.com/
Design Firm
Ari Feldman

Ari's homepage has a cool, subdued look achieved through the use of soft, muted colors. The centerpiece image has real life and energy.

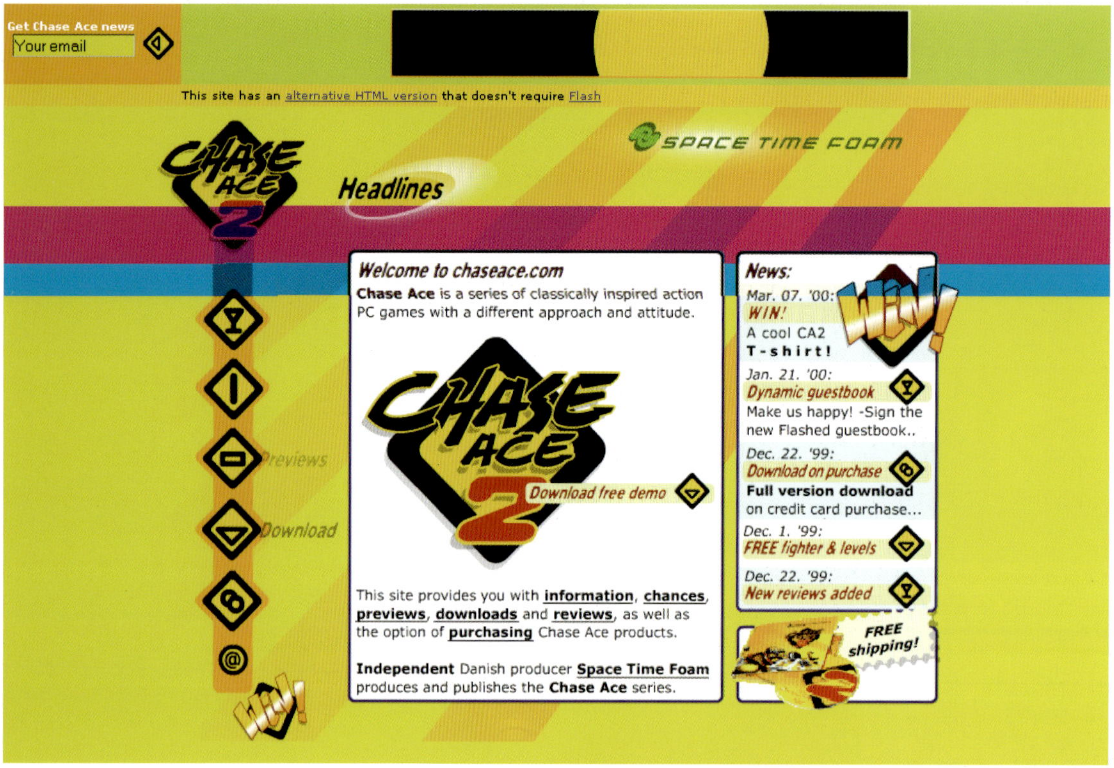

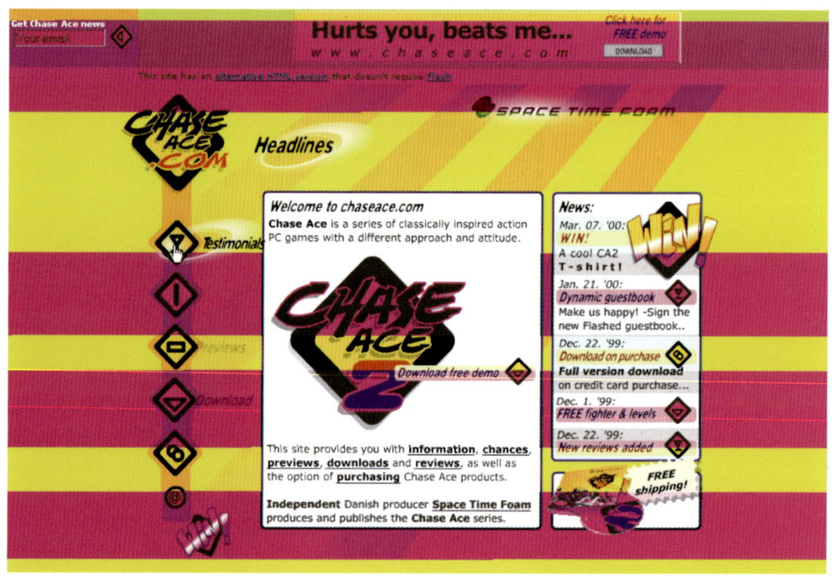

Title
chase ace
URL
www.chaseace.com/
Design firm
chase ace

There is a lot happening on this splashpage. The six buttons create movement, and the logo keeps your attention focused squarely on the product. The strong color scheme is somewhat jarring but fits in with the overall street-sign design.

Spider monkey

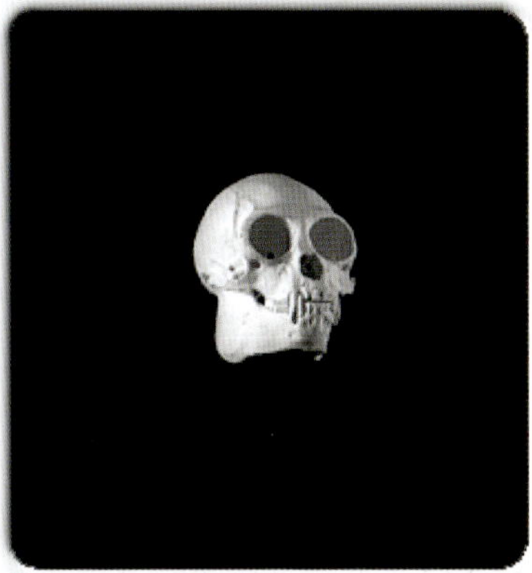

Ateles paniscus: **Distribution** 0mm

Modern anthropoid primates are divided into two infraorders, the Platyrrhini (New World monkeys, such as the spider monkey at left) and the Catarrhini (Old World monkeys, apes, and humans). These groups probably diverged sometime during the Oligocene epoch (38-23 million years ago) and differ in a number of respects. The Platyrrhini retain more primitive features than the Catarrhini. For example, the Platyrrhini have three premolars, which is closer to the ancestral condition than the two premolars found in the Catarrhini.

The infraorder Catarrhini is divided into two superfamilies: the Cercopithecoidea (Old World monkeys) and the Hominoidea (apes and humans). These superfamilies diverged during the Miocene (23-5.5 million years ago).

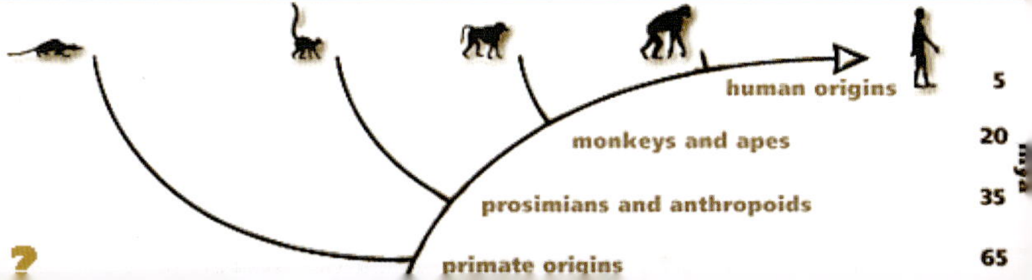

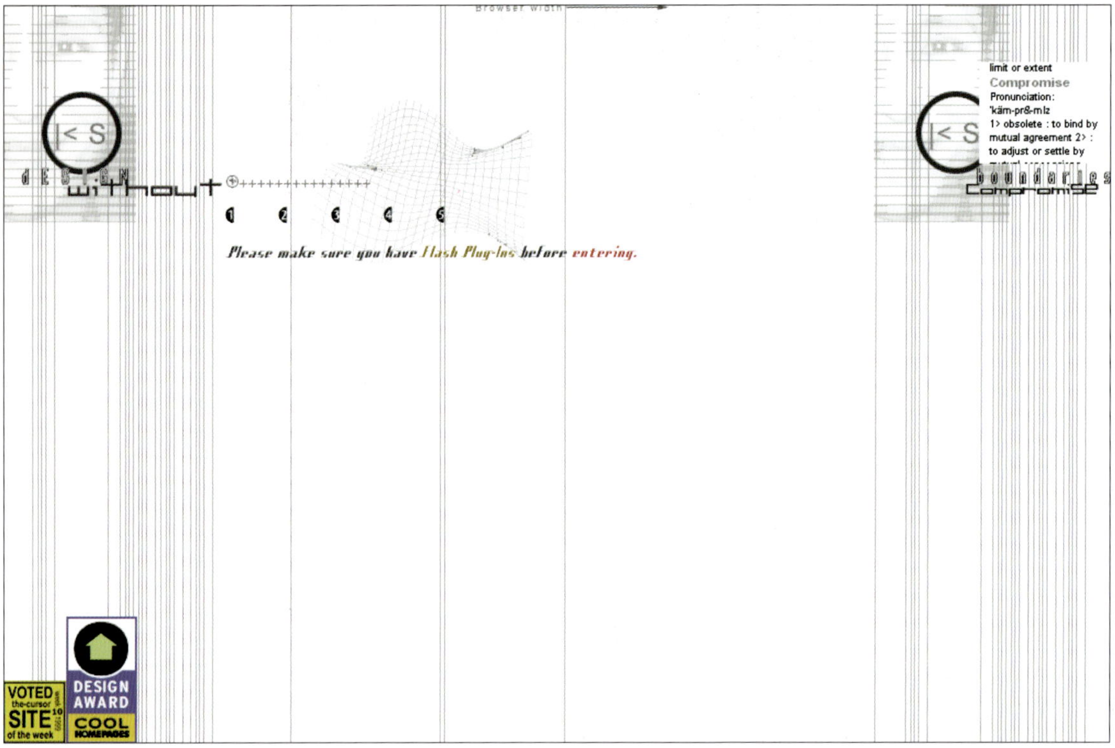

Title
Kim Seng
URL
www.freshdsign.com/kimseng
Design Firm
Consortio Inc.
Designer
Kim Seng

Flash provides plenty of movement. The simple black-and-white design has eight animated buttons and lines that follow the cursor around the screen.

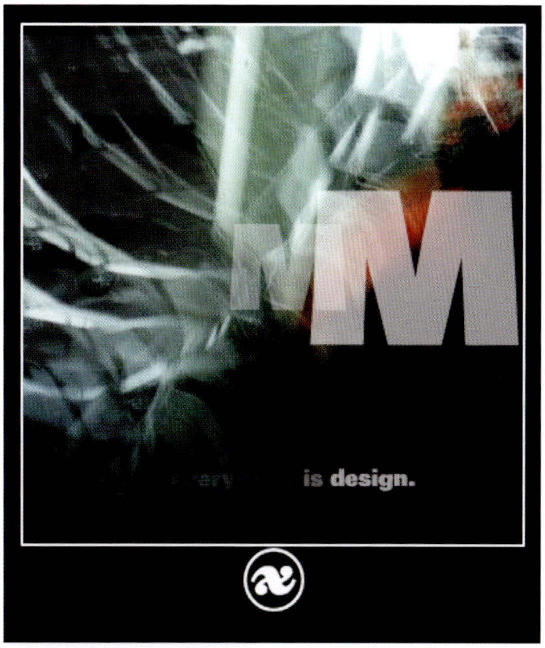

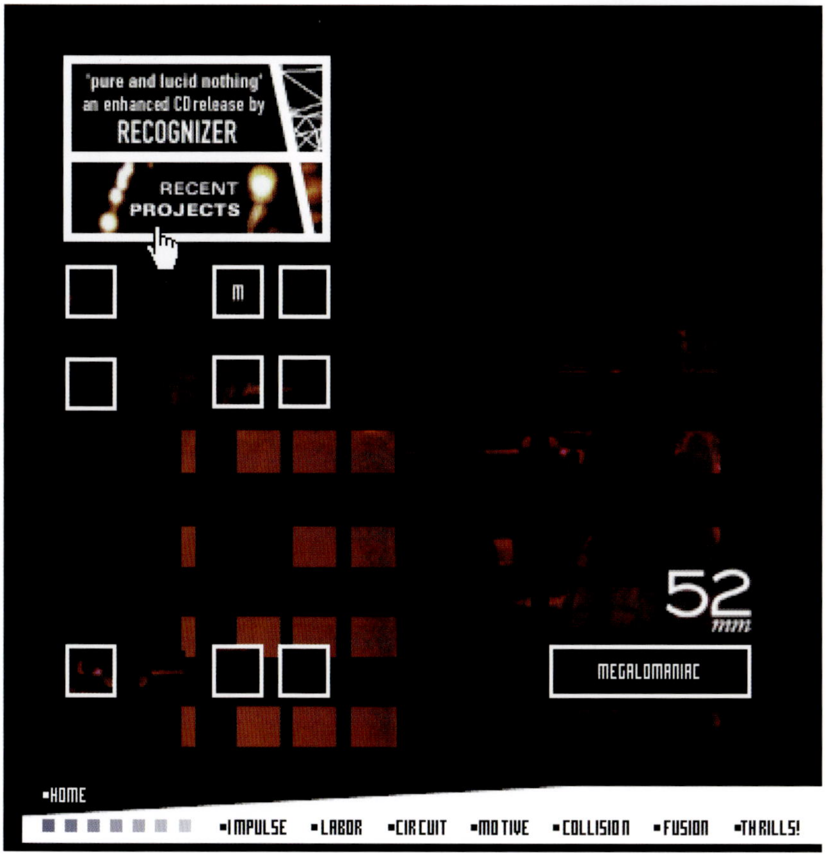

Title
52 mm
URL
www.52mm.com/
Design firm
52 mm

This homepage is a Flash pop-up window that contains a few small buttons along the bottom and a sparse, black design that introduces the site very well.

Title
D+CON/trol
URL
www.decontrol.com/deconv1/
Design Firm
D+CON/trol

Eight buttons that don't explain anything tell you all you need to know about this site in a Flash pop-up window. If you would like to hear about D+CON/trol's philosophy, click on the "What's the deal?" button.

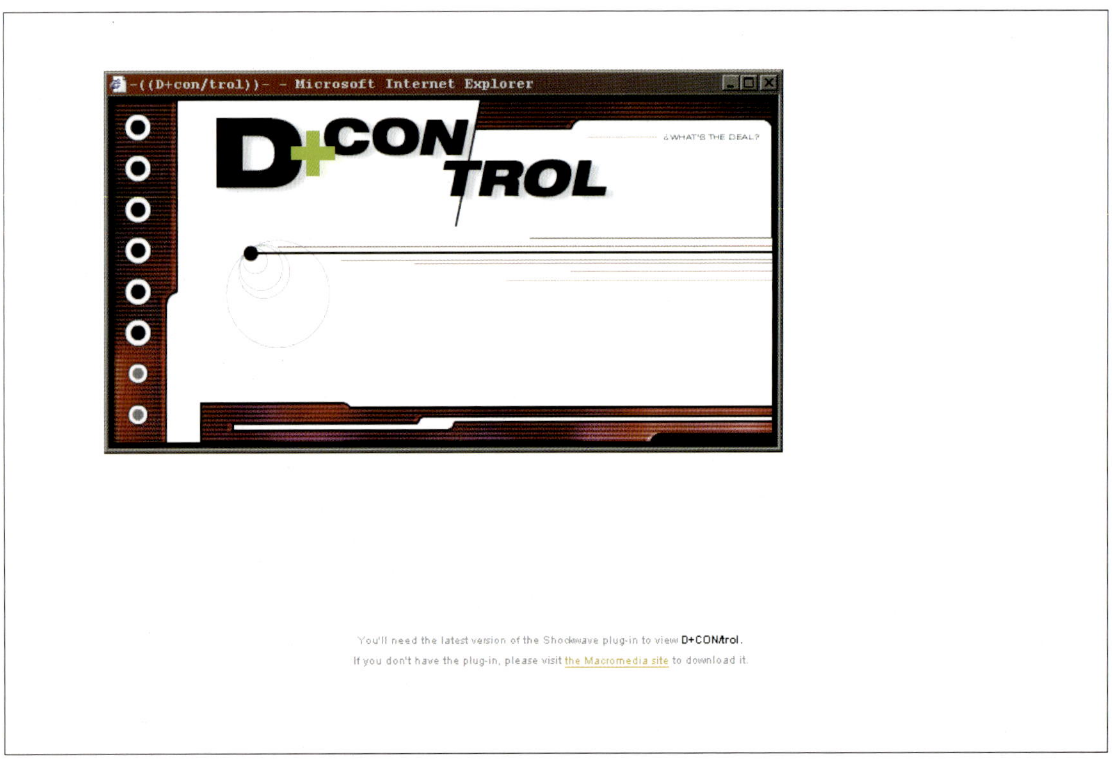

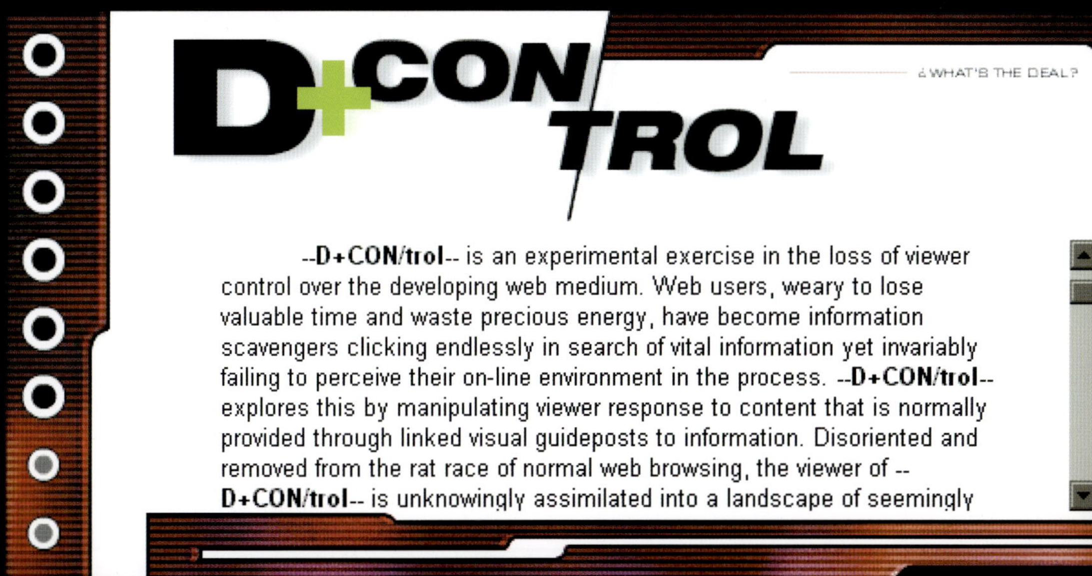
D+CON TROL
¿WHAT'S THE DEAL?
--D+CON/trol-- is an experimental exercise in the loss of viewer control over the developing web medium. Web users, weary to lose valuable time and waste precious energy, have become information scavengers clicking endlessly in search of vital information yet invariably failing to perceive their on-line environment in the process. --D+CON/trol-- explores this by manipulating viewer response to content that is normally provided through linked visual guideposts to information. Disoriented and removed from the rat race of normal web browsing, the viewer of --D+CON/trol-- is unknowingly assimilated into a landscape of seemingly

Title
Neostream
URL
www.neostream.com/
Design firm
Neostream Interactive

One of the greatest interfaces on the Web, the Neostream site features five buttons with iconic illustrations that pop into the window on mouse-over. A great international site because the images make language unnecessary.

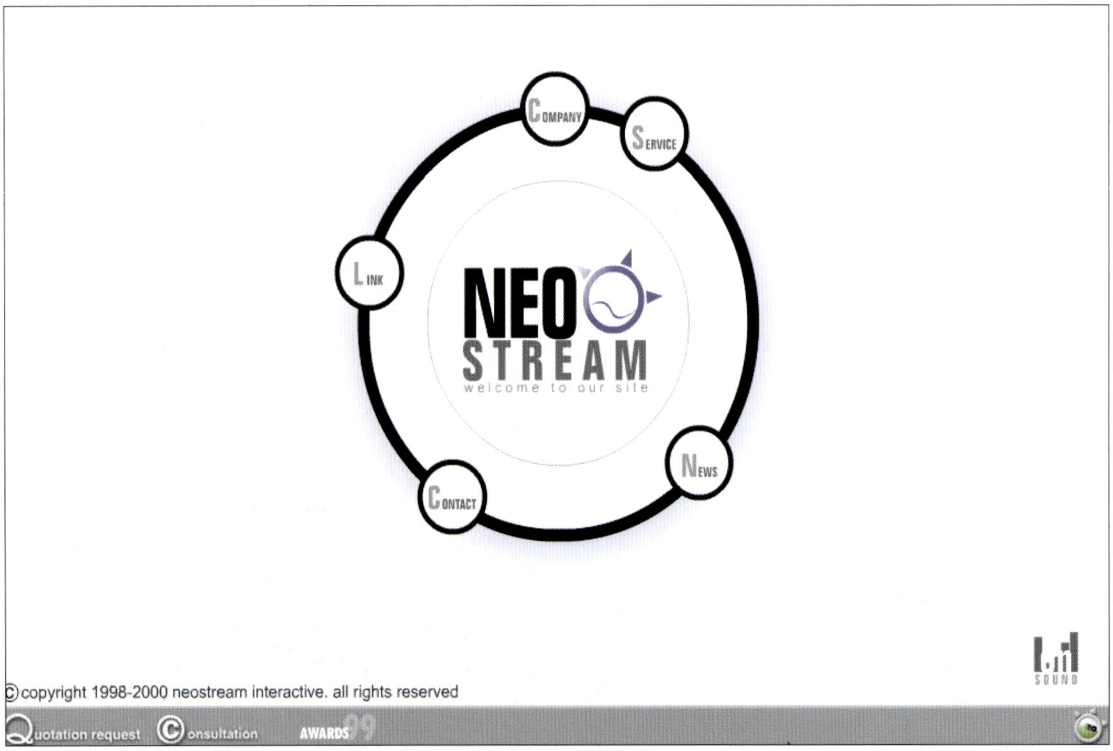

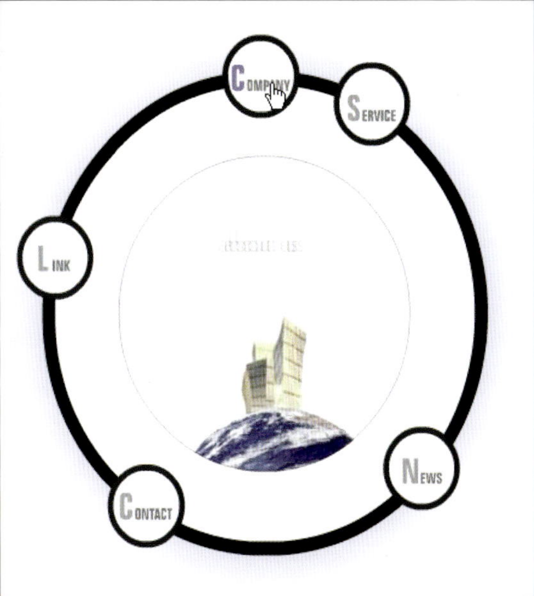
Company
Service
Link
News
Contact

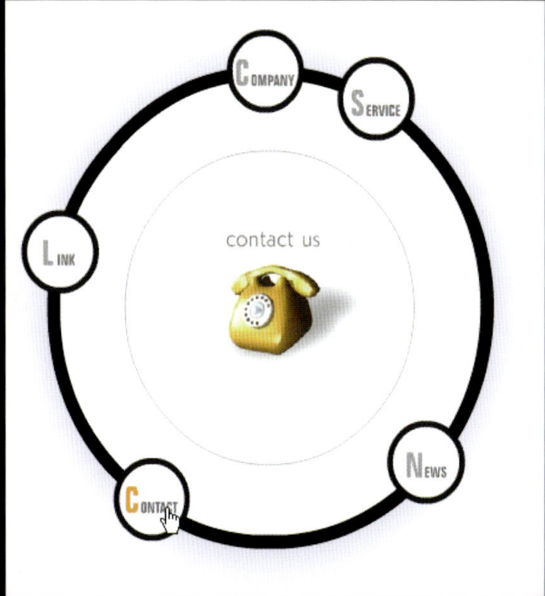
Company
Service
Link
contact us
News
Contact

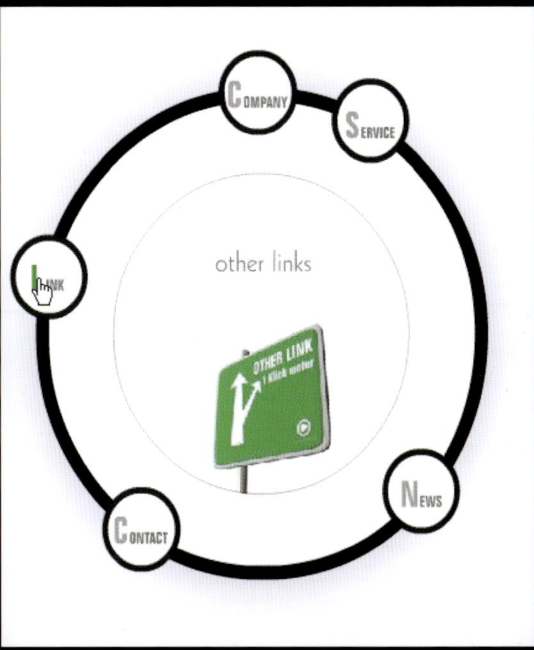
Company
Service
Link
other links
OTHER LINK
News
Contact

Title
Juxt Interactive
URL
www.juxtinteractive.com/
Design Firm
Juxt Interactive

Juxt Interactive makes possibly the best use of color on the Internet. The blue, yellow, black, and white create a scheme unlike any on the web, and the sound on this site is extraordinary. Good movement created using Flash and clear navigation buttons complete an excellent design.

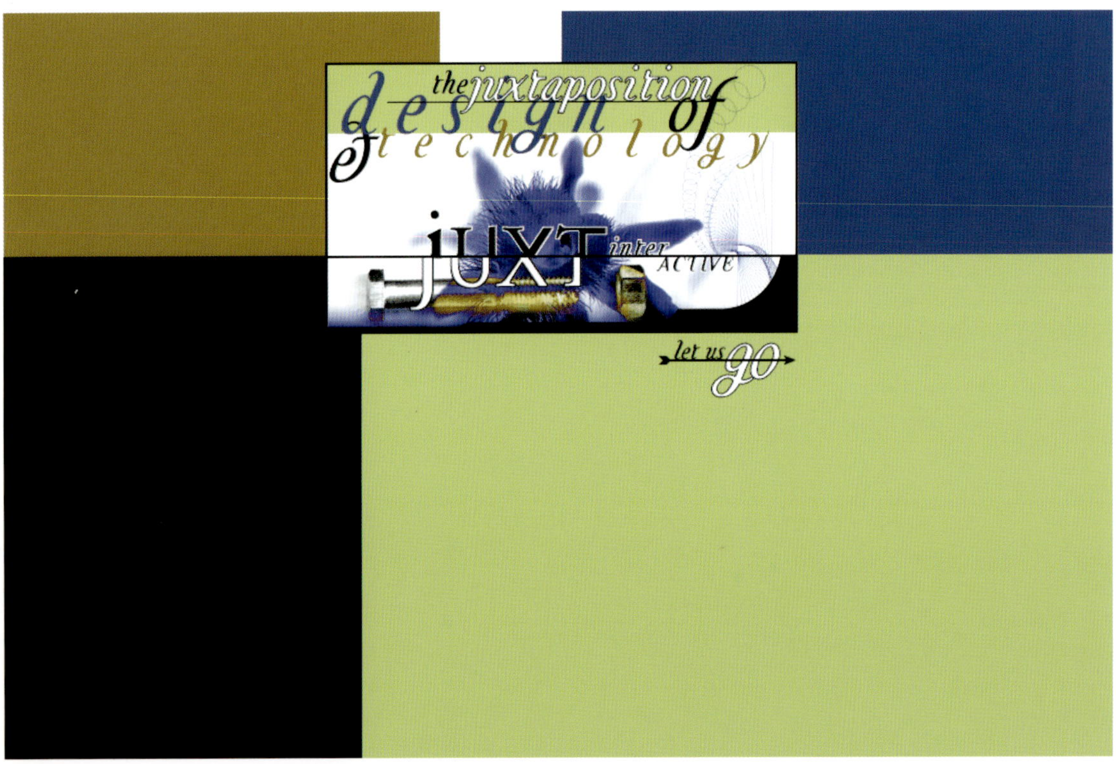

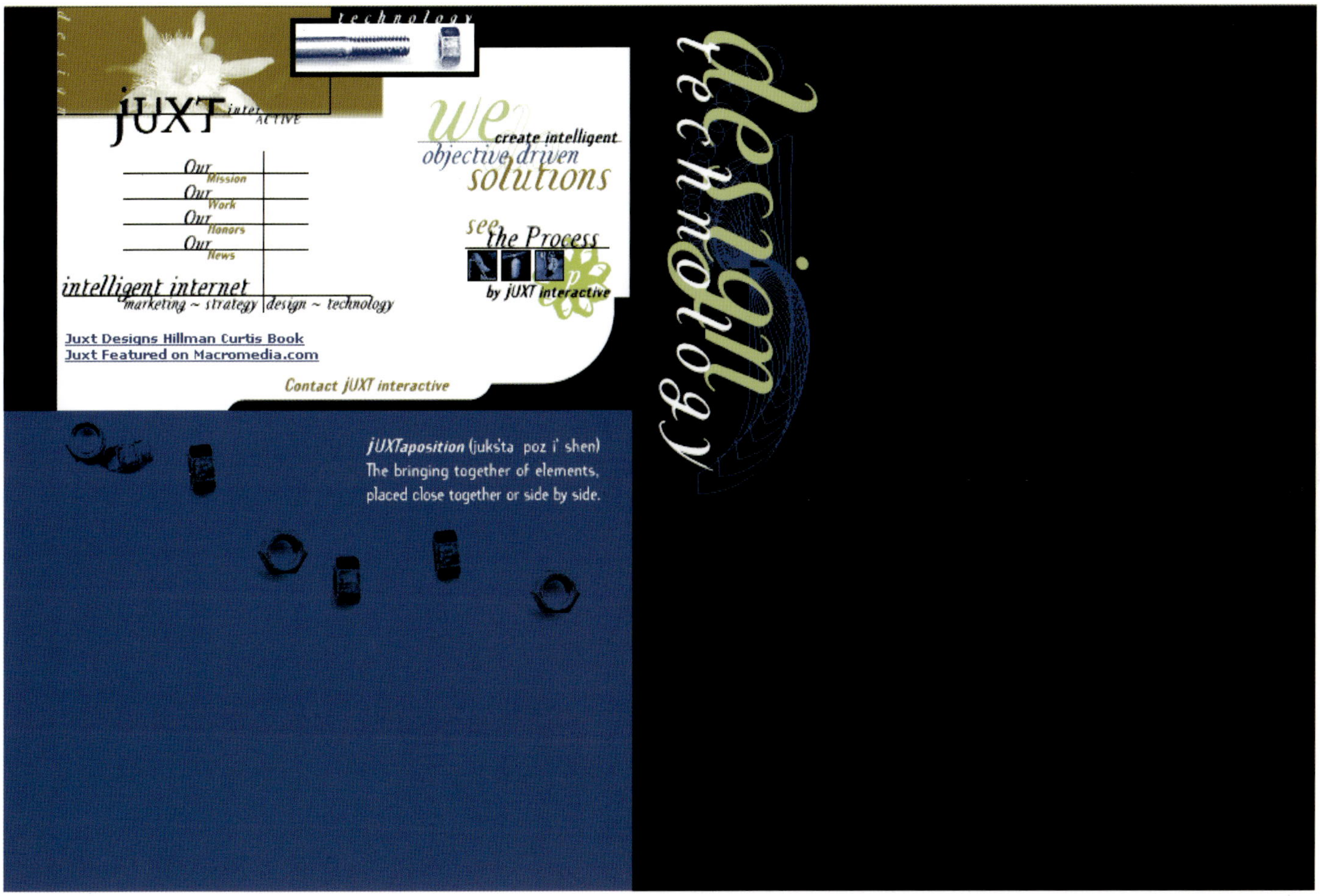
technology
jUXT interACTIVE
we create intelligent
objective driven
solutions
Our Mission
Our Work
Our Honors
Our News
see the Process
by jUXT interactive
intelligent internet
marketing ~ strategy design ~ technology
Juxt Designs Hillman Curtis Book
Juxt Featured on Macromedia.com
Contact jUXT interactive
jUXTaposition (juks'ta poz i' shen)
The bringing together of elements,
placed close together or side by side.
design
technology

Title
Ideo
URL
www.ideo.com/
Design Firm
Ideo

Ideo has great colors on their homepage, particularly the underused colors like greens and oranges.

Find a project

Go

About IDEO | What we do | Recent clients | Project archives | Contact us | Press

About IDEO

IDEO creates products, services and environments for companies pioneering new ways to provide value for their customers. Drawing on twenty years of experience in the field of innovation and design, IDEO defines and develops new futures for industry leaders and start-ups alike.

Having created thousands of products for hundreds of clients, IDEO brings unmatched experience to the process of strategic innovation, from conception through production.

Roll over an area for more information

- Strategic Services
- Human Factors and Ergonomics
- Concept Development
- Environments
- Industrial Design
- Interaction Design
- Mechanical Engineering
- Electrical & Software Engineering
- Manufacturing Support

- IDEO Healthcare
- Skyline

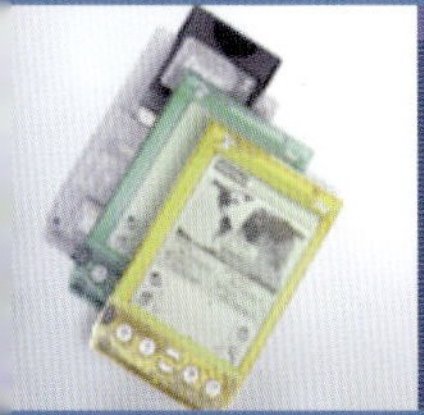

Handspring Visor

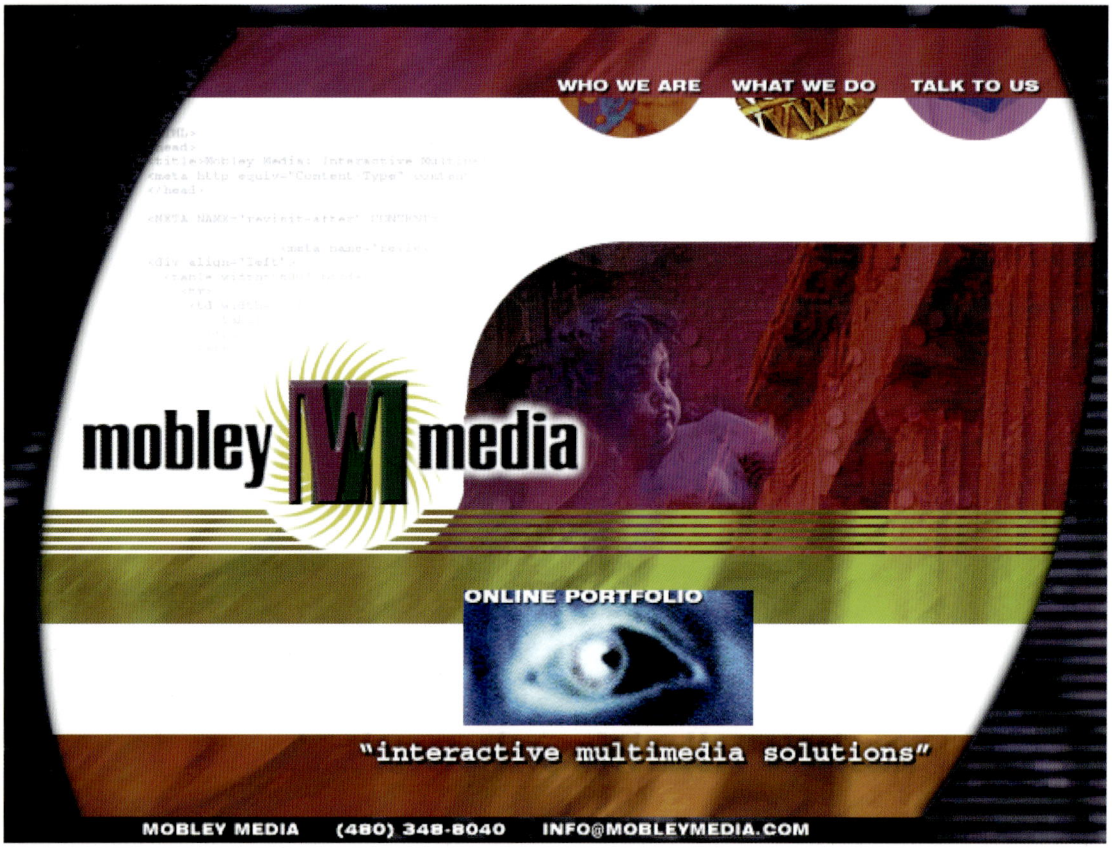

Title
Mobley Media
URL
www.mobleymedia.com/
Design Firm
Mobley Media
Designer
Margie Mobley

Great use of color and a lush background illustration make this homepage noteworthy. Simple buttons make the site easy to navigate as well.

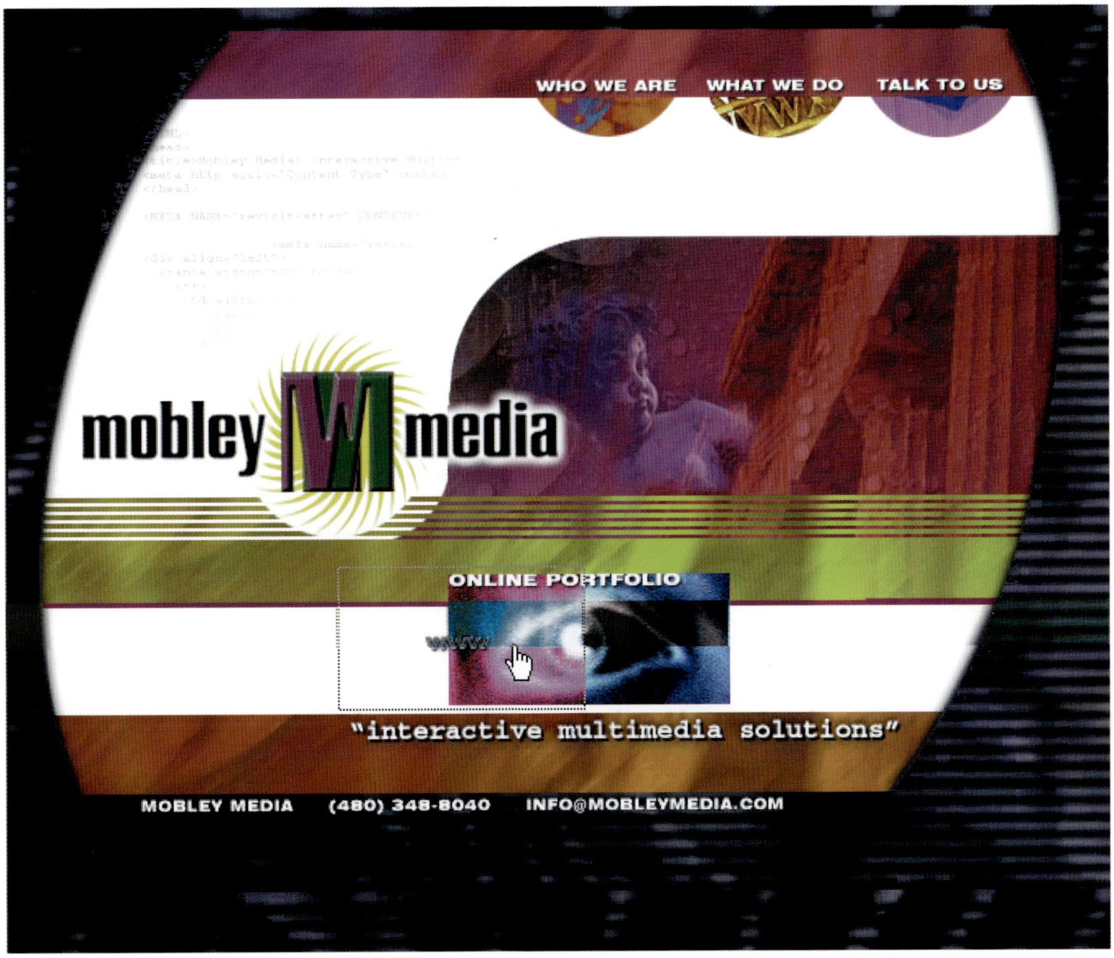
WHO WE ARE
WHAT WE DO
TALK TO US
mobley media
ONLINE PORTFOLIO
"interactive multimedia solutions"
MOBLEY MEDIA
(480) 348-8040
INFO@MOBLEYMEDIA.COM

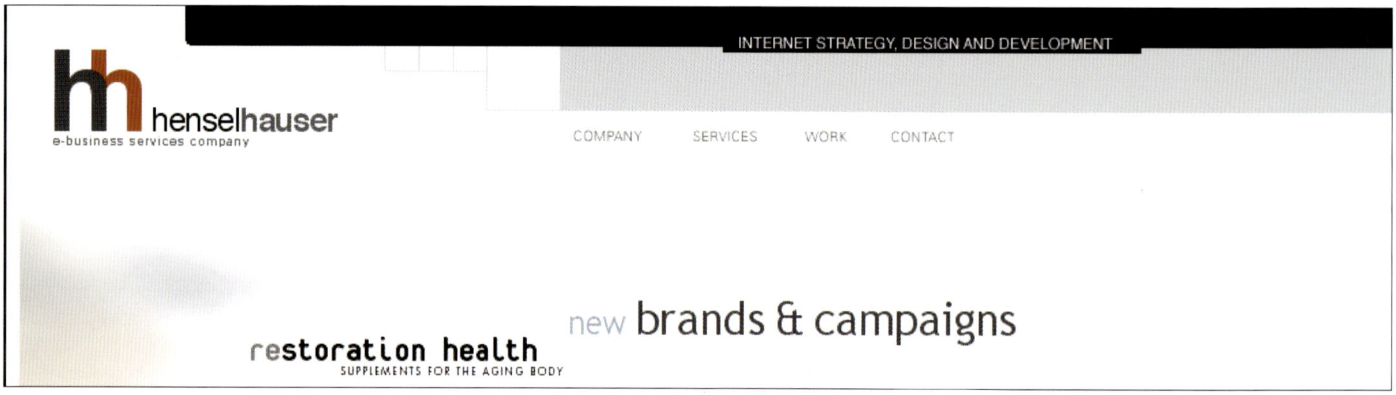

Title
Hensel Hauser
URL
www.henselhauser.com/
Design Firm
Hensel Hauser
Designer
Todd Hauser

This splashpage features some of Hensel Hauser's work. This page is radically different from the rest of the site; thus, it conveys the feeling of a gateway page.

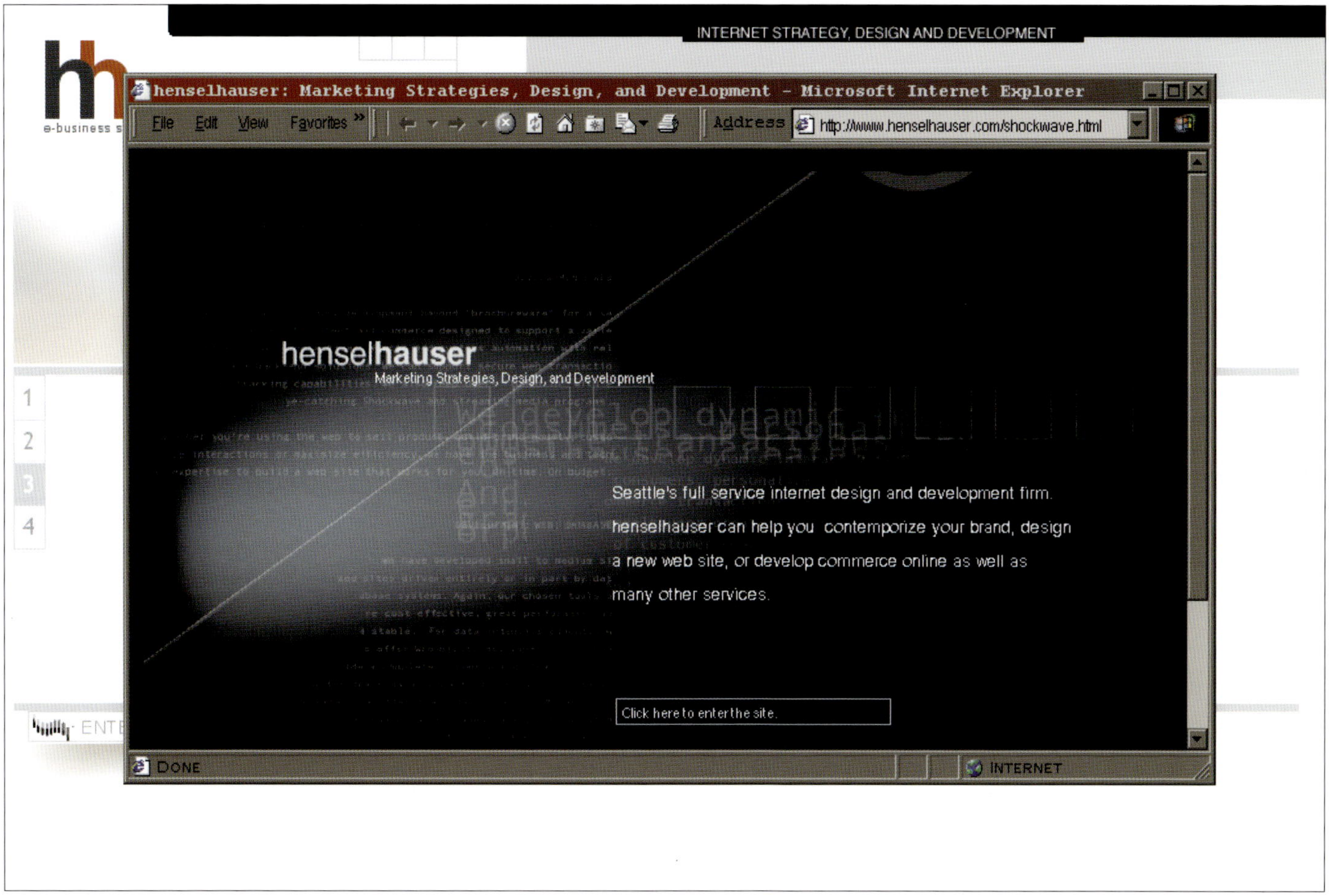

INTERNET STRATEGY, DESIGN AND DEVELOPMENT
henselhauser: Marketing Strategies, Design, and Development - Microsoft Internet Explorer
File Edit View Favorites
Address http://www.henselhauser.com/shockwave.html
henselhauser
Marketing Strategies, Design, and Development
Seattle's full service internet design and development firm.
henselhauser can help you contemporize your brand, design
a new web site, or develop commerce online as well as
many other services.
Click here to enter the site.
DONE
INTERNET
1
2
3
4

Directory

3D Reality.net
346 Park St. Suite C
Birmingham, MI 48009
info@3dreality.net
www.3dreality.net/main.htm

52 mm
12 John St. #10
New York, NY 10038
info@52mm.com
www.52mm.com/

ABI Mouldings
3815 32nd St. NE
Calgary, AB T1Y 7C1
CANADA
markd@abimouldings.com
www.abimouldings.com/

Andy Lim
(Embedded Wireless Labs)
andy@artdirectors.com
andy.artdirectors.com/

Ari Feldman
316 East 55th St. Apt. 3C
New York, NY 10022
ari@arifeldman.com
www.arifeldman.com/

Asmussen Interactive
Stubbekebingv 98B, 108
4800 Nykebing F.
DENMARK
ja@nethow.dk
www.turtleshell.com/asm

Chase Ace
(Petergrafik/Space Time Foam)
Brigadevej 28A 2th
DK2300 KBH S.
DENMARK
peter@petergrafic.dk
www.chaseace.com/

Clint Baker
3222 Cherry Hill Ave. NW C1
Washington D.C. 20007
me@clintbaker.com
www.clintbaker.com

The Cultural Landscape Foundation
1909 Que St. NW 3rd Floor
Washington D.C. 20009
info@tclf.org
www.tclf.org/

D+CON/trol
(One Ten Design Inc.)
820 N La Brea Ave.
Los Angeles, CA 90038
contact@onetendesign.com
www.decontrol.com/deconv1/

Designgraphik
1011 Columbine Dr. Apt. 1B
Frederick, MD 21701
mike@designgraphik.com
www.designgraphik.com/

E3 Directiv
311-1040 15 Ave. SW
Calgary, AB T2R-0S5
CANADA
kontakt@e3directiv.com
www.e3directiv.com/

Envision Interactive
987 University Ave. Suite #22B
Los Gatos, CA 95032
insight@interactive.com
www.envisioninteractive.com/

Euro.runner SrL
Via Massarenti 190
40138 Bologna
ITALY
info@eurorunner.com
www.eurorunner.com/

Eye 4 U Active Media
Schwere-Reiter-StraBe 35
Haus 7
D-80797 Munich
GERMANY
info@eye4u.com
eye4u.com/home/index.htm

The Firm List
2 Phillips St. #2
Boston, MA 02114
matte@firmlist.com
www.thefirmlist.com/main.htm

First 9 Months
(12 South.com)
209 10th Ave S Suite 340
Nashville, TN 37203
joe@12south.com
www.first9months.com/

Gary Venter Architect
1001/12 Ithaca Road
Elizabeth Bay NSW 2011
AUSTRALIA
gary@gary.net.au
www.gva.net.au/

Gobler Toys
1 Oak Ave.
Tuckahoe, NY 10707
iragobler@goblertoys.com
www.goblertoys.com/

Goran Design
Somborska 35
25260 Apatin
YUGOSLAVIA
goran@gorandesign.com
www.gorandesign.com/index.html

Heavy.com
141 West 41st St. 3rd Floor
New York, NY 10036
www.heavy.com/

Hensel Hauser
1867 E. Hamlin St.
Seattle, WA 98112
todd@henselhauser.com
www.henselhuaauser.com/

Human Evolution
Department of Anthropology
University of California,
Santa Barbara campus
Santa Barbara, CA 93106
walker@sscf.ucsb.edu
www.sscf.ucsb.edu/~hagen/crania/

Iconiklastique Design Klinik, LLC
1932 South Halstead St.
Studio 502
Chicago, IL 60608
e-mail@ida-a-ok.com
www.ida-a-ok.com/

Ideo
700 High St.
Palo Alto, CA 94301
scott@ideo.com
www.ideo.com/

Insomnious, Ltd
P.O. Box 300
London, HA1 3SP
UNITED KINGDOM
nosleep@insomnious.com
www.insomnious.com/

IShopHere.com
722 Randle Ave.
Nashville, TN 37202
ccormichael@ishophere.com
www.ishophere.com/

Jason Felix
227 Judah St.
San Francisco, CA 94122
fistsoffury@hotmail.com
www.jasonfelix.com/newinterface.html

Jon Duarte Communications
3230 Overland Ave.
Suite 124
Los Angeles, CA 90034
design@jonduarte.com
www.jonduarte.com/

Juxt Interactive
858 Production Place
Newport Beach, CA 92663
info@juxtinteractive.com
www.juxtinteractive.com/

KaBloom
200 Wildwood Ave.
Woburn, MA 01801
dyshar@kabloom.com
www.kabloom.com/

Kim Seng
(Consortio Inc.)
27 Jalan Aman Teluk Air Tawar
13050 Butterworth, Penang
WEST MALAYSIA
ks_74@yahoo.com
www.freshdsign.com/kimseng

King Led Comics
2975 Barclay Ave. #7
Montreal, Quebec H5S 1J9
CANADA
kingled@sympatico.ca
www3.sympatico.ca/kingled/

KVAD.com
Langarinden 407
N-5132 Nyborg
NORWAY
vatne@online.no

Lambie-Nairn
Greencoat House
Francis St.
London SW1P 1DH
UNITED KINGDOM
www.lambie-nairn.com/flash_go.html

Me Company
14 April Studios
Charlton Kings Road
London NW5 ZSA
UNITED KINGDOM
info@mecompany.com
www.mecompany.com/

Mediamax
Doukissis Plakentias 12
15127 Melissia
Athens
GREECE
info@mediamax.gr
www.mediamax.gr

MKSite
(Massimo Kunstler)
128 Via Salaria
00198 Rome
ITALY
mk@mksite.com
mksite.com/

Mobley Media
7702 E. Doubletree Ranch Rd. #300
Scottsdale, AZ 85258
mmobley@mobleymedia.com
www.mobleymedia.com/

The Multimedia Group
499 St. Kilda Rd.
Melbourne VIC 3004
AUSTRALIA
info@themmgroup.com
www.themmgroup.com/

Neostream Interactive
Gate 4 Bldg. 1
Riverside Corporate Park
105 Delhi Road
North Ryde NSW 2113
AUSTRALIA
www.neostream.com/

Netgraphic
(Audiobox Ulanghanzepte)
Iterdhurmstr 68
CH-8005 Zurich
SWITZERLAND
stagars@audiobox.com
www.netgraphic.ch/

Ntouch
(Random Media)
Prospect Row
87 Lansdowne Drive
London E8 3EP
UNITED KINGDOM
victor@randommedia.co.uk
ntouch.linst.ac.uk/

02 Studios
987 University Ave #22B
Los Gatos, CA 95032
spencer@o2studios.com
www.o2studios.com/

Obliviance
11 Ewart Road
London SE23 1AY
UNITED KINGDOM
rmiller@obliviance.ndirect.co.uk
www.obliviance.ndirect.co.uk/

Online Interview with Randall Larson
687 79th St.
Lino Lakes, MN 55014
gonzoz@mn.mediaone.net
people.mn.mediaone.net/gonzoz

Party Flights
(Amphion Multi Media)
Vlaase KAAI 43
2000 Antwerp
BELGIUM
www.party-flights.com/

Petergrafik
(Petergrafik/Space Time Foam)
Brigadevej 28A 2th
DK2300 KBH S.
DENMARK
peter@petergrafic.dk
www.petergrafik.dk/

Pod New Media Ltd
49 Mount Pleasant
London WC1X 0AE
UNITED KINGDOM
info@p-o-d.co.uk
www.p-o-d.co.uk/

Raging Pixels
1000 Conestoga Rd. c-266
Rosemont, PA 19010
www.ragingpixels.com/flash/ragingpixels.htm

Resonant SrL
Piazza G Mazzini 27
00195 Rome
ITALY
mail@resonant.it
www.resonant.it/

Ricochet Creative Thinking
310-126 York St.
Ottawa, ON KIN 5T5
CANADA
www.ricochetcreativethinking.co/

Rullkötter AGD Werbung + Design
Kleines Heenfeld 19
D-32278 Kirchlengern
GERMANY
info@rullkoetter.de
www.rullkoetter.de/

Solemates
(The Marketing Store)
920 9th St. 2nd Floor
Sacramento, CA 95814
www.centuryinshoes.com/home.html

Staticlife
(Todaiflunk No-Media Network)
409 Lomita Ave. #227
Glendale, CA 91204
sun@staticlife.com
www.staticlife.com/box/interface1998/index_ie.html

Superesc
130 Sandpiper Way NW
Calgary, AB
CANADA
calvin@superesc.com
www.superesc.com/

Synewave
414 Garden St. #7
Hoboken, NJ
synewave@aol.com
www.synewave.com/

Timeticker
(Zwernemann)
Gaisbuehlstrasse 2
79725 Laufenberg
GERMANY
martin@zwernemann.de
www.timeticker.com/

Typographic
443 South Cochran Ave. #201
Los Angeles, CA 90036
jimmy@typographic.com
www.typographic.com/

Wireless Knowledge LLC
6215 Ferris Square
San Diego, CA 92121
gbeneke@wirelessknowledge.com
www.wirelessknowledge.com/

Wojtek
(Perplex GMBH)
Sauerbruchtstr 1
97375 Munich
GERMANY
wojtek@wojtek.com
www.wojtek.de/

Wolvesburrow Productions
2045 Wildwood Lane
Hanover Park, IL 60103
heydt@wolvesburrow.com
www.wolvesburrow.com/

Yenz
via Mercadante 8
20124 Milan
ITALY
yenz@yenz.com
www.yenz.com/

Yster
(SLB Interactive)
Stranden 3a
Aker Brygge
NORWAY
oystein@slb.no
yster.just.nu

Zedmain
761 E 16th Ave #303
Eugene, OR 97408
zedvox@hotmail.com
members.tripod.com/zedvox/zedmain.htm

About the Author

Richard Karl Danielson is a freelance writer and artist living in Cambridge, Massachusetts. He has produced live theater, cut a record of his own songs, and written for a variety of media–electronic and print. He studied history and writing at Marlboro College. He is a Web designer by avocation and is fascinated with the current Internet revolution. He is currently producing a short movie for the Web and writing a book on cinematography.